YOUR CHARACTER
MATTERS

Includes a Study Guide with Questions for
Group Discussion or Personal Reflection

YOUR CHARACTER
MATTERS

10 Character Traits God Calls Every
Christian Leader to Demonstrate

J. A. JOHNSON
B. K. WOOLSEY

We enjoy hearing from our readers. Please contact us at www.anekopress.com/questions-comments with any questions, comments, or suggestions.

www.genesiscollegeandseminary.com

Your Character Matters

© 2025 by J. A. Johnson and B. K. Woolsey

All rights reserved. Published 2025.

Cover Designer: J. Martin

Handshake Image: Dalle

Editor: Paul Miller

Aneko Press

www.anekopress.com

Aneko Press, Life Sentence Publishing, and our logos are trademarks of

Life Sentence Publishing, Inc.
203 E. Birch Street
P.O. Box 652
Abbotsford, WI 54405

RELIGION / Leadership

Paperback ISBN: 979-8-88936-496-2

eBook ISBN: 979-8-88936-497-9

10   9   8   7   6   5   4   3   2   1

Available where books are sold

Contents

Introduction

When someone says to you, "Tell me about your-self," how do you respond? Most people begin with their name and what they do for a living: "My name is Carl, and I'm the executive pastor at New Horizons Fellowship." While this is a typical answer, it doesn't get to the heart of who the person is.

Your job is what you do. Your character is who you are. You may have an important title and an indispens-able set of leadership skills. You may be really good at your job – maybe even amazing. But without godly character, nothing else matters. If you have poor char-acter, there will be a limit to your usefulness to God, your church, and your followers.

Much too often we hear about respected and influ-ential Christian leaders who fall. They may have cha-risma, vision, and a notable following, but when their weak character and compromising morals come to light, they fall into disgrace, harm the believers who looked to them for spiritual guidance, and damage the reputation and testimony of Christ's church to the watching world. Leaders with poor character point to a broader theme that Scripture regularly confirms: character shapes conduct. Specifically, godly character produces godly conduct; ungodly character produces ungodly conduct.

The truth that character shapes conduct is evident from the beginning of humankind. *The serpent was more crafty* than all other beasts of the field, and the first record of his conduct was to challenge God and corrupt man (Genesis 3:1-6).

What a contrast to Noah, who just three chapters later gets a commendation rarely ascribed to those in the Old Testament: *Noah was a righteous man, blameless in his generation. Noah walked with God* (Genesis 6:9). Although just as much a part of fallen humanity, Noah's reverent fear and faith shaped his godly character, and he *found favor in the eyes of the* LORD and *became an heir of the righteousness that comes by faith* (Hebrews 11:7).

God cares about our character. While man is enamored by outward appearances, God looks upon the heart. He values a clean heart and godly character more than any amount of righteous work (Psalm 51:16-17; Isaiah 1:12-20; 29:13; 66:2). And remarkably, He is able through His Spirit to regenerate the corrupt, restore the fallen, and reassure the feeble.

Leadership Greatness

While many leaders look to enhance their knowledge, skills, and abilities in the hope of learning better methods of church leadership and management, God is looking for something much more substantial, as noted succinctly by E. M. Bounds: "The Church is looking for better methods; God is looking for better men."[1] God is far more interested in who you are and what you can be than in what you do and how much you achieve.

God measures greatness much differently than we do. "It's not great talents or great learning or great preachers that God needs," Bounds says, "but men great in holiness, great in faith, great in love, great in fidelity, great for God. . . . These can mold a generation for God."[2]

This book is about becoming great for God – not necessarily *doing* great things for Him, but *being* the kind of person who is guided by the Spirit (Galatians 5:24-25) and living in daily repentance and dependence on God (1 John 1:9; 2:1; 3:6). If you will pursue godliness and prioritize your character above your methods, God will bless your efforts and your effectiveness, and the harvest will increase for His glory.

How the Book Is Organized

The goal of this book is to provide a firm understanding of the spiritual qualifications required to lead God's people. The book is for all Christian leaders who have a servant's heart, who want to lead the church God's way, who want to model Christlike behavior, and who are willing to make changes in their lives to be great for God.

---

1   E. M. Bounds, *Power Through Prayer* (Chicago: Moody Publishers, 2009), 17.

2   Bounds, *Power Through Prayer*, 21.

We examine ten intertwining dimensions of character that come from the apostle Paul's letters to Timothy and Titus (1 Timothy 3:2-13; Titus 1:5-10). Paul makes it clear to his two protégés that those who lack these character traits have no business leading others. These traits are nonnegotiable, and they serve to organize the chapters of this book.

Paul calls all Christian leaders to be:

1. Blameless

2. Humble

3. Servants to Their Family

4. Trustworthy

5. Disciplined

6. Upright

7. Gentle

8. Hospitable

9. Lovers of Good

10. Holy

These dimensions of character do not come naturally to us but develop as we are conformed to the image of Christ, our example of flawless character. His lifestyle on earth fully represented all that God is without any defect or blemish. As you strive toward Christlikeness so that *Christ is formed in you* (Galatians 4:19), God will give you the grace and desire to grow in His will. You can be assured that *he who began a good work in you will bring it to completion at the day of Jesus*

Christ (Philippians 1:6). You can also be assured that growth in godly character is the key to fruitful ministry (2 Peter 1:5-7, 10).

Character Trait Assessment

The Character Trait Assessment (CTA) located in the back of the book is a tool to help you evaluate the strengths and weaknesses of your character. Before beginning chapter one, complete the CTA and ask two other people who know you well to complete it on your behalf. Ask them for honest feedback, which will help you discern potential areas of growth. Please don't ignore the CTA or disregard its value. It will help you pinpoint character deficiencies that you may not be aware of.

Study Guide

A study guide is provided at the end of this book to help you review, assess, and apply what you have learned in this book. We pray this will give you concrete ways of opening up to God's transforming work in your life and ministry. The questions in this guide can be used for group study or personal reflection.

May God bless you as you continue to grow in Christlikeness and be all that He wants you to be. Before you begin this journey, ask God for His guidance and help.

Heavenly Father, as I read the following pages, I invite Your Holy Spirit to examine who I am. I don't want to be a person who lacks character in any area of my life. I long to be transformed into the image of Your Son. My heart is pliable. My spirit is teachable. Please transform me. In Jesus' name I pray. Amen.

Chapter 1

Be Blameless

B e blameless, sinless, without fault, above reproach – perfect in all your ways. Jesus is the *lamb without blemish or spot* (1 Peter 1:19). Jesus lived a blameless life, and we are also *to be found by him without spot or blemish* (2 Peter 3:14). The Bible calls us to:

- *be holy and blameless before him* (Ephesians 1:4)

- *be pure and blameless for the day of Christ, filled with the fruit of righteousness that comes through Jesus Christ* (Philippians 1:10-11)

- *be blameless and innocent, children of God without blemish in the midst of a crooked and twisted generation* (Philippians 2:15)

Blamelessness is the calling of every believer, and leaders in particular are to demonstrate it. It's no wonder that being above reproach heads the list of Paul's qualifications for church overseers. Paul tells Timothy, *The saying is trustworthy: If anyone aspires to the office of overseer, he desires a noble task. Therefore an overseer must be above reproach* (1 Timothy 3:1-2). Similarly, Paul begins his instructions to Titus by saying that *an overseer, as God's steward, must be above reproach* (Titus 1:7).

To be above reproach (Greek: *anepileptos*) means to be blameless or unrebukable, so there must not be any true charge or accusation that can be brought against a leader. His life and conduct must not give cause to taint the gospel or the church's testimony to the world. He isn't *arrogant or quick-tempered or a drunkard or violent or greedy for gain* (Titus 1:7). Instead, he demonstrates a life that is shaped by the gospel, living in such a way that brings honor, not disrepute, to God.

All eyes are on church leaders. We model to those in our congregations how to live and behave, setting *the believers an example in speech, in conduct, in love, in faith, in purity* (1 Timothy 4:12). It is imperative, therefore, that we:

- practice what we preach

- obey laws (that don't contradict the gospel)

- tell the truth

- avoid gossip

- stand strong in faith amid trials and tribulations

- live a godly lifestyle in the community, at church, and at home

Paul doesn't just say that an overseer must be above reproach. He says, *As God's steward, . . . be above reproach*

(Titus 1:7). The Greek word for steward (*oikonomos*) means the holder of a commission in the service of the gospel. It is a high calling, a huge responsibility, and we can't take it lightly.

There are many intertwining dimensions of character in Paul's letters to Timothy and Titus, and the first one, blamelessness, sets the tone for all of them. As you seek to be a leader who stewards God's household, being above reproach is nonnegotiable. Following are several ways to cultivate blamelessness in your life and ministry.

1. Pursue Godliness

It is easy for church leaders to get caught up in the work of ministry and neglect the work the Holy Spirit is trying to do to make them more godly. The pursuit of godliness must be our highest priority. Paul's continual emphasis on godly living highlights its importance. In 1 Timothy alone, Paul says:

- *lead a peaceful and quiet life, godly and dignified in every way* (2:2)

- *train yourself for godliness* (4:7)

- *godliness is of value in every way* (4:8)

- *show godliness to their own household* (5:4)

- *teaching that accords with godliness* (6:3)

- *godliness with contentment is great gain* (6:6)

- *pursue righteousness, godliness, faith, love, steadfastness, gentleness* (6:11)

When you live a God-centered life that is submitted to the will of the Holy Spirit, godly living is the result. Because the church is God's household, its stewards must attend to the church as He would. They are representatives of God (Ephesians 4:11-14; Hebrews 13:7), and the church itself is a reflection of God's character. Therefore, it is vital for God's household to be led by godly leaders.

2. Be Godly Even When No One Is Looking

What kind of person are you even when no one is watching you? The answer to this question reveals your true character. You and I can put on a facade in front of others and even have the *appearance of godliness* (2 Timothy 3:5), but the real you and the real me surface when we're alone with our private thoughts and behaviors.

King David resolved to walk with integrity in his private life. He said, *I will ponder the way that is blameless. . . . I will walk with integrity of heart within my house; I will not set before my eyes anything that is worthless* (Psalm 101:2-3). Job also made a decision to walk with personal integrity: *I have made a covenant with my eyes not to look lustfully at a young woman* (Job 31:1 NIV). If we are only godly in front of others, we are no better than the Pharisees whose actions were merely external – for others to see – and not from their hearts, which were far from God (Mark 7:6).

To be people of integrity, we must focus on the inmost self, or what David calls the *inward being* and *secret heart* (Psalm 51:6). God delights in integrity in the internal place of our lives that no one sees – that place where we are most honest with ourselves. Paul told Timothy, *The aim of our charge is love that issues from a pure heart and a good conscience and a sincere faith* (1 Timothy 1:5). Only you and God know if your heart is pure, if your conscience is good, and if your faith is real.

In Psalm 19, David rejoiced in the law of the Lord, which exposes all of the hiding places of the soul. He said that the commands of the Lord are more desired than gold (v. 10), for they serve as a warning that there are sins lurking in his heart (vv. 11-12). David asked God to cleanse him from hidden faults: *Keep back your servant also from presumptuous sins; let them not have dominion over me! Then I shall be blameless, and innocent of great transgression* (v. 13). He then offered a prayer that is relevant for all who seek to walk in integrity in their private lives: *Let the words of my mouth and the meditation of my heart be acceptable in your sight, O LORD, my rock and my redeemer* (v. 14).

When we resolve to be godly when no one is looking, we will not only have a clear conscience before God, but we will also produce the fruits that are required of us as leaders. Obedient and godly actions flow from our inward being. Character always shapes conduct.

3. Ask God to Show You Gaps in Your Character

Christian leaders are to keep a close watch on

themselves, guarding their own spiritual and moral purity (Acts 20:28; 1 Timothy 4:16). If you do not guard yourself, you will become more and more numb to sin's deceitfulness. There are some *whose consciences are seared* (1 Timothy 4:2), and their consciences are no longer guides for godly living. They have become hardened to the truth and have no remorse for doing wrong. Examining yourself daily (2 Corinthians 13:5) will keep open communication and fellowship with the Lord, providing opportunity to prevent sin so that you will not fall into the snare of the devil.

You may already know your areas of weakness – those places in your life in which you are most vulnerable, or gaps in your character. Or maybe you're unaware of gaps in your character. Invite the Holy Spirit to reveal to you any area that is dishonoring to God. David prayed, *Search me, O God, and know my heart! Try me and know my thoughts! And see if there be any grievous way in me, and lead me in the way everlasting!* (Psalm 139:23-24).

As you ask God to show you where you fall short in regard to ethical and moral purity, He will reveal to you places of unlikeness to Christ and will create in you a clean heart (Psalm 51:10). That is His part. What is our part? We are to put off the old self, which belongs to our *former manner of life and is corrupt through deceitful desires,* and we are *to be renewed in the spirit of [our] minds* (Ephesians 4:22-23). This enables us to think in new and godly ways so we can put on *the new self, created after the likeness of God in true righteousness and holiness* (Ephesians 4:24).

4. Establish Character Guardrails

Character guardrails are steps you take to keep yourself from being in a position where you might be likely to sin or be accused of improprieties. Guardrails are a way of keeping watch on yourself (Ephesians 4:16). We see guardrails on roads that are built next to cliffs. These guardrails protect us from sure disaster, preventing us from veering off the road. In the same way, character guardrails prevent us from veering off the path of godliness.

John Maxwell is a leadership expert and bestselling author who has grown in popularity and fame. He says that one of his potential pitfalls is to live in the glow of admiration. To help him focus on his integrity and not his image, he asks himself three questions that serve as guardrails to keep him on track:

1. *The question of consistency.* Am I the same person no matter who I am with?

2. *The question of choices.* Do I make choices that are best for others even when another choice would benefit me?

3. *The question of credit.* Am I quick to recognize others for their efforts and contributions to my success?[3]

I set up formal guardrails for my life when I was forty-nine years old. I realized that half of my life was surely over, and I wanted to ensure that the rest of my life would be devoted to living a life of godly character.

---

3   John Maxwell, *Developing the Leader Within You 2.0* (Nashville: HarperCollins Leadership, 2018), 62.

I created a covenant of fifty resolutions that detailed the type of person I would be. For example, during the first half of my life I leaned on crutches such as alcohol to escape stress or to manage hardships. So resolution number forty-one identifies this as a potential pitfall:

> #41. Resolved to run to Jesus when trials come, not to self-medicate for escape.
>
> *With unwavering devotion, I look to Jesus as the one to run to when I am weary or burdened. Alcohol, cannabis, pills, and porn temporarily numb the pain while deepening the wound, but Jesus heals the pain and binds the wounds of the broken-hearted (Psalm 147:3). So I will run to Jesus when tough times try to rob my joy.*

I wish I would have created such guardrails when I was much younger. If I would have focused on my character and would have drawn lines that were never to be crossed, it would have saved me and others from a world of pain and sorrow.

Do you have any formal guardrails in place to keep you on a godly course? You might ask yourself some questions like John Maxwell does, or maybe it's time to write your own set of resolutions with regard to the type of person and leader you will be. Whatever you decide, be intentional about keeping watch on yourself.

5. Set Up an Accountability System

When you're seeking to cultivate blamelessness in your life, accountability is essential. You need oversight to ensure that you are making godly decisions, conducting yourself in a manner befitting the gospel, and living above reproach. You can't afford to be insulated, and accountability is one of the best ways to guard against it.[4]

After I composed my fifty resolutions, I asked a couple of my close friends to hold me accountable to the covenant I had made. I asked them to call me out on anything that indicated I was veering off the path of righteousness.

As you enter an accountability relationship with someone, there are several things to keep in mind:

1. Be sure the person is of your gender (unless the accountability person is your spouse).

2. Be sure the person is someone you trust.

3. Be real. Accountability systems only work if you have the courage and humility to be honest and transparent. If not, you'll be a phony, which is obviously bad character.

4. Give the person permission to speak into your life. You'll only benefit from an accountability relationship if the one holding you accountable feels free to be candid with you.

5. Check your pride. Don't let your ego be a stumbling block to your own growth. It can be easy

---

4   Brad Lomenick, *The Catalyst Leader* (Nashville: Thomas Nelson, 2013), 147.

to get defensive when others point out faults and wrongdoings. If you truly want to make positive changes, remember that corrections are not attacks; they are opportunities to improve. Respond with appreciation and use their feedback as a means of grace to make you more like Christ.

Every leader needs accountability. No one is too spiritual or too moral to make mistakes or poor choices. Accountability is a guardrail to help you stay on the straight and narrow path of godliness so that you may be a leader who is above reproach.

As you strive for blamelessness in your life and ministry, (1) pursue godliness, (2) be virtuous when no one is looking, (3) ask God to show you gaps in your character, (4) establish character guardrails, and (5) set up an accountability system. If you're a leader who is blameless, you will be an example that others want to follow. You will earn the trust of those you lead, and this will position you to make a difference in their lives. And it gets even better. Those who are not yet a part of your church will see that you're the real deal, and your godly testimony of righteousness will make you a believable representative of the gospel to the world.

Jesus Is Our Model for Blamelessness

Jesus *knew no sin* (2 Corinthians 5:21). *He committed no sin, neither was deceit found in his mouth* (1 Peter 2:22). Even Pilate, the Roman ruler who had the authority to condemn and punish Jesus, said to the crowds, *I find no guilt in this man* (Luke 23:4). Pilate restated this truth two additional times (Luke 23:14, 22). As Christian leaders who are conformed to the image of Christ, those same words that Pilate spoke of Jesus should be spoken of us.

Because Jesus *bore our sins in his body on the tree, that we might die to sin and live to righteousness* (1 Peter 2:24), we can be severed from all ties to sinfulness. Jesus *is able to keep [us] from stumbling and to present [us] blameless before the presence of his glory with great joy* (Jude 1:24).

Don't strive to be blameless on your own. While there are ways to cultivate blamelessness in your life, rely on God's power through faith in Christ to shape you into a person and leader who is above reproach.

Chapter 2

Be Humble

Have you ever worked for someone who is full of himself? I have. Me. As a pastor, I have been my own boss. I have been that leader who thinks he knows everything – that leader whose ideas are always right and best. But praise God that the pride of that leader continues to be chipped away as he seeks to be transformed more and more into the image of Christ.

Paul knew that there was no place for pride in the leadership of the church. He told Titus that an overseer of a church *must not be arrogant* (Titus 1:7). Arrogant people believe they are superior to everyone else. They think they have the best ideas, the best methods, and the most talent. They also tend to one-up others. If you can do something, they can do it better. If you've made an accomplishment, well, they've made a better one.

Paul says we are to one-up each other, but not in showing superiority: *Outdo one another in showing honor* (Romans 12:10). A leader honors those he serves when he places their needs above his own.

Humility (Greek: *tapeinophrosune*) is having a modest opinion of your importance or status. Humble people:

- don't think too highly of themselves
- don't think they're better than everyone else
- don't brag about their accomplishments
- focus on others and rarely talk about themselves
- deflect praise, willingly passing on credit to others
- are not above doing lowly tasks
- are honest about their flaws and failures

In Philippians 2, Paul tells us how to practice humility among the community of believers. From his discussion we can extract at least four marks of a humble leader.

1. Humble Leaders Are Not Selfishly Ambitious

Paul says, *Do nothing from selfish ambition* (Philippians 2:3). Selfishly ambitious people are bent on advancing their agenda at any cost. It's okay to have ambition, but your ambition must not be self-serving. Paul was ambitious, but notice that in his address to the Ephesian elders his ambition is aimed at serving others and God:

You yourselves know how I lived among

*you the whole time from the first day that
I set foot in Asia, serving the Lord with all
humility and with tears and with trials
that happened to me through the plots of
the Jews; how I did not shrink from declar-
ing to you anything that was profitable, and
teaching you in public and from house to
house, testifying both to Jews and to Greeks
of repentance toward God and of faith in our
Lord Jesus Christ. And now, behold, I am
going to Jerusalem, constrained by the Spirit,
not knowing what will happen to me there,
except that the Holy Spirit testifies to me in
every city that imprisonment and afflictions
await me. But I do not account my life of
any value nor as precious to myself, if only I
may finish my course and the ministry that I
received from the Lord Jesus, to testify to the
gospel of the grace of God.* (Acts 20:18-24)

Paul gave his life to help others believe and receive the
gospel so that their lives would be championed by its
power. His focus was on serving others and Jesus. This
is the humility in action that we are called to demonstrate in our own lives.

2. Humble Leaders Are Not Hungry for Honor

Paul wrote, *Do nothing from . . . conceit* (Philippians 2:3).
Those who are conceited desire to be esteemed by
others. The word conceit "connotes being hungry for

honor, recognition, and status."[5] There is no place for such hunger in the life of a Christian, let alone in the life of a Christian leader. If we have the profound joy and consolation that comes from Christ, we should not need the approval of others.

3. Humble Leaders Consider Others Better than Themselves

Not only are we to do nothing from selfish ambition or conceit, but Paul added, *but in humility count others more significant than yourselves* (Philippians 2:3).

Prideful people look down on others. They believe they're better than everyone else, always comparing themselves to others. C. S. Lewis said, "It's the comparison that makes you proud; the pleasure of being above the rest."[6] This pleasure is manifest when we feel we have:

- a more prestigious college degree than others

- a better paying salary than our counterparts

- better behaved children than others

- a larger church than our friends who are pastors

- a more fit body than others

- a bigger house, a better car – the list goes on and on

---

5   Timothy Keller, *Gospel in Life Study Guide* (Grand Rapids: Zondervan, 2010), 188.

6   C. S. Lewis, *Mere Christianity* (New York: Macmillan, 1952), 109-110.

If we have the mindset that we're better or that we need to be better than everyone, we will never be able to count others more significant than ourselves; we'll be too wrapped up in our own significance.

Prideful leaders make much of themselves. In Greek mythology, Narcissus was a young man who saw his reflection in a pool and fell in love with himself. A prideful person tends to be narcissistic, admiring and even idolizing his or her strengths, abilities, and talents. Such a person minimizes and devalues the giftings and contributions of others. As Christian leaders, we must not have even a trace of narcissism in our lives. To help you evaluate your opinion of yourself, honestly answer the following questions.

To what extent do I:

- feel superior to those who work for me?

- fail to regularly acknowledge the debt I owe to my mentors and to others?

- denigrate the motives and accomplishments of others?

- expect others to serve me or defer to me?

- put my own success ahead of the success of others?

- behave in ways that seem egocentric to those around me?[7]

Questions like these help us check ourselves to see if we have feelings of superiority.

---

7   John Maxwell, *Developing the Leader Within You 2.0* (Nashville: HarperCollins Leadership, 2018), 51.

4. Humble Leaders Serve Their Followers

Paul wrote, *Let each of you look not only to his own interests, but also to the interests of others* (Philippians 2:4). It is natural for us to look to our own interests, but we must take the same level of concern we have for ourselves and apply it to the interests of those we serve. A good question to ask yourself is, "Do I make decisions that are best for others even when another choice would benefit me?"[8] Like Paul, we must *try to please everyone in everything [we] do, not seeking [our] own advantage* (1 Corinthians 10:33).

When our decisions and actions are self-serving, we violate our charge to humble service. We're called to look to the interests of others and to serve those we lead, following the example of Christ, who *came not to be served but to serve, and to give his life as a ransom for many* (Matthew 20:28).

Becoming Humble

Humble leaders are not selfishly ambitious or hungry for honor. They consider others better than themselves, and they serve their followers, putting the needs of others above their own. These are marks of humility that Paul calls us to demonstrate.

Selflessness is the thread that weaves these marks of humility together. As we become more and more selfless, it will be reflected in every area of our leadership. We will deflect glory and praise away from ourselves

---

8   Maxwell, *Developing the Leader*, 62.

and onto God. We will be willing to do menial tasks. We will make time for those who can do nothing for us. We'll even be transparent about our weaknesses and shortcomings, not feeling compelled to impress others. We will be selfless because our Savior was selfless and because we want our lives and ministries to reflect His. Christlike leaders are humble.

John the Baptist was such a leader. He was the prophesied *Elijah who is to come* (Matthew 11:14), of whom Jesus said, *Among those born of women there has risen no one greater* (Matthew 11:11). Yet John didn't consider himself as one who was worthy to even carry Christ's sandals (Matthew 3:11). When we read about his ministry, we discover his refusal to receive accolades or praise. Instead, he said, *He must increase, I must decrease* (John 3:30). May that be said of us as well.

Jesus Is Our Model of Humility

Humility is cultivated in our lives as we emulate the character of Christ, who was humble in all His ways. He was born in humble circumstances – in a feeding trough for animals (Luke 2:12). He had a humble job, working as a carpenter with His earthly father (Mark 6:3). He even lived in a humble city. When Phillip urged Nathanael to follow Jesus, Nathanael asked, *Can anything good come out of Nazareth?* (John 1:46). Jesus humbly served others, as clearly demonstrated when He stooped to His knees to wash His disciples' feet (John 13:5).

The epitome of Christ's humility is shown in his crucifixion. Paul wrote:

> *Have this mind among yourselves, which is yours in Christ Jesus, who, though he was in the form of God, did not count equality with God a thing to be grasped, but emptied himself, by taking the form of a servant, being born in the likeness of men. And being found in human form, he humbled himself by becoming obedient to the point of death, even death on a cross.* (Philippians 2:5-8)

This passage gives us a glimpse of Christ's humility. He:

- gave up His rights and status

- laid aside His privileges

- became a servant

- was obedient to God in the midst of suffering

- humbled Himself on the cross – a humiliation reserved for the most notorious criminals

Follow Christ's example and clothe yourself with humility (1 Peter 5:5). As you do, God will shower you with His blessings – guaranteed. He *gives grace to the humble* (1 Peter 5:5) and promises to exalt whoever humbles himself (Matthew 23:12).

Chapter 3

Be a Steward of Your Family

Do you cheat on your spouse by using pornography or by having sexual thoughts about someone who is not your spouse? Do you rob your children of opportunities to grow in spiritual maturity by not addressing their bad attitudes or disrespectful comments? Have you shown that you can manage your family by establishing godly expectations and traditions?

If you struggle to be a spiritual guide to the people you love the most, you will be crippled in your efforts to lead others in God's church. Your home is the proving ground for your character.

Being a faithful steward of your family might seem more like a responsibility than a character attribute, but Paul mentions the management of one's household as a requirement for eldership in God's household. Paul began his discussion of family matters by telling husbands to be *the husband of one wife* (1 Timothy 3:2). While there is a lot of theological discussion surrounding the meaning of this verse, we can be certain that it prohibits marital infidelity.[9] Paul also told Timothy how an elder is to steward his family. Paul said, *He must manage his own household well, with all dignity keeping his children submissive, for if someone does not know how to manage his own household, how will he care for God's church?* (1 Timothy 3:4-5).

Spiritual leadership begins at home. We are to be godly spouses and parents if we are to be qualified to take care of God's people. Here are several ways to cultivate your character at home:

1. Selflessly Love Your Spouse

Wives are to love their husbands and submit to them, respecting them as the spiritual leaders of the home (Titus 2:4-5; Ephesians 5:22-24). The word "submit" might seem overbearing in today's secular society, but Paul is not advocating a self-centered, authoritarian exercise of power. Nor is he saying that the wife is unequal to her husband. Paul is merely describing God's order of relationships. The head of the wife is her husband, the head of the husband is Christ, and the head of Christ is God (1 Corinthians 11:3). The wife isn't inferior to

---

9 The meaning of *husband of one wife* is widely debated. Does it mean that single men or divorced people can't be elders? Was Paul referring to polygamists? For a discussion of several views regarding the meaning of this phrase, see the note on 1 Timothy 2:2-3 in the *ESV Study Bible* (Wheaton: Crossway, 2008). No matter what view you hold, one thing we can be sure of: God prohibits any kind of marital unfaithfulness (Hebrews 13:4).

her husband, just as Christ isn't inferior to His Father. Jesus and His Father are equal in deity and attributes (John 5:19; 10:30; Colossians 1:15). Jesus is, however, submissive to His Father (John 5:36; 10:37; 14:28, 31).

Biblical submission is a beautiful phenomenon. The wife places herself under her husband's protection and provision, and the husband takes care to serve her emotional, physical, and spiritual needs. Wives love their husbands by submitting to them, and husbands love their wives by following the example of love set by Christ. Paul said, *Husbands, love your wives, as Christ loved the church and gave himself up for her* (Ephesians 5:25).

Husbands have an enormous responsibility. Just as Jesus gave Himself up for the church through His sacrificial death on the cross, husbands are to be willing to lay down their lives for their wives. That might result in literal sacrifice, but it really means the sacrifice of self. Egos, preferences, and desires all take a back seat so the husband can put his wife's best interests first. Husbands are bound by love to ensure that their wives find their marriage to be a source of rich fulfillment and joyful service to the Lord.[10]

Husbands and wives are equal to one another, but with different roles. When the wife submits to her husband and he fulfills his sacrificial responsibility to his wife, they display godliness and bring glory to God in their marriage union.

---

10   S. M. Baugh, Ephesians Study Notes in the *ESV Study Bible* (Wheaton: Crossway, 2008). See note on Ephesians 5:25, p. 2272.

As you nurture a loving relationship with your spouse, here are some expectations to set for yourself:

- Don't keep secrets or hide anything from your spouse.

- Be considerate of your spouse's feelings.

- Put your spouse's needs above your own.

- Show appreciation even for the small things.

- Express your love daily, letting your actions speak louder than your words.

- Remember that you're on the same team; if someone "wins" an argument, the relationship loses.

- Don't be alone with a person of the opposite sex.

- Be slow to anger, quick to forgive.

Finally, husbands, make every effort to ensure that your wife knows she is loved and protected. Be loyal to her and help her know that she is secure in your relationship. Wives, be sure to help your husband feel needed, admired, and appreciated. As you treat each other with selfless love and respect, you can be sure that it will be reciprocated.

2. Practice Sexual Purity

There are many ways to demonstrate integrity in your marriage relationship, but following these three are essential for every leader:

(1) Quit using pornography today. Porn is a secret sin that ensnares and devours many church leaders. They might think they're being faithful to their spouses since they're not having extramarital sex, but they are, in fact, cheating on their marriage partner, having affairs of the heart. Jesus said that a man who looks lustfully has already committed adultery in his heart (Matthew 5:28).

William Mounce discusses the widespread usage of pornography among pastors and Christian leaders. One of his friends is a Christian counselor who offers group therapy for pastors and elders with sexual addictions. Mounce's friend said, "You can't face the issue of pornography in the church until you face the issue in the leadership."[11]

This is an attempt to face the issue. If you struggle with pornography or other sexual addictions, get help today. Help can come in many forms, including professional counseling or by confiding in someone you trust and asking that person to hold you accountable to be morally pure.

Sharing struggles and asking for help requires humility. It requires courage. If a person with a sexual addiction chooses not to confront it, the Bible assures us that there will be serious consequences (Ephesians 5:5). No sin remains unhidden (Luke 12:2-3). The writer to the Hebrews said, *Let marriage be held in honor among all, and let the marriage bed be undefiled, for God will judge the sexually immoral and adulterous* (Hebrews 13:4).

---

11   William Mounce, "Biblical Leadership in the Pastoral Epistles," p. 7. Accessed October 5, 2021. www.biblicaltraining.org.

The Greek word for "sexually immoral" is *pornos*, which refers to one who engages in any sexual conduct outside of marriage. Anyone who uses pornography is sexually immoral and is subject to the disciplinary judgment of God.

Leaders have a greater responsibility to be sexually pure. Everyone will give an account to God (Hebrews 13:17), but God judges teachers and leaders *with greater strictness* (James 3:1). With greater responsibility comes greater expectations.

(2) Keep your eyes only on your spouse. "You can look, but not touch" is a saying of the world, but it is not applicable for people in God's kingdom. "Looking" needlessly opens your heart and your imagination to someone who isn't your marriage partner. Job pursued righteousness in all areas of his life, including moral purity. He made a covenant with his eyes not to look lustfully at someone who was not his spouse (Job 31:1). Making such a pledge requires intentionality. It requires a decision. Decide today that your heart belongs to God and that your eyes belong only to your spouse.

(3) Find sexual delight in your spouse. King Solomon said, *Drink water from your own cistern* and *Rejoice in the wife of your youth* (Proverbs 5:15, 18). This is a call to enjoy the spouse God has given you. Any sexual desires you have must be expressed with your marriage partner. A husband is to let his wife's breasts fill him at all times with delight as he is intoxicated in her love (Proverbs 5:19). Proverbs 5 gets a little

steamy, emphasizing the truth that your spouse is a gift from God and will bring you lifelong satisfaction and companionship.

3. Establish Godly Expectations for Your Family

Paul tells Timothy that church overseers must know how to manage their households and, with all dignity, to keep their children submissive (1 Timothy 3:4). Paul is not suggesting that parents rule their homes with iron fists, nor is he advocating draconian measures. Rather, he is calling for respect in the family and for children to follow the rules of the home.

Establish nonnegotiable expectations in your home. Insist that your children:

- Obey you and your spouse.

- Respect you and your authority. (Don't allow them to usurp your authority through talking back, sassing, or arguing with you.)

- Practice kindness with everyone in the home.

- Tell the truth.

- Complete their chores.

- Have good attitudes.

- Demonstrate godly behavior inside and outside the home.

- Attend church services and fellowship gatherings with you.

Becoming a godly manager of your household carries the added benefit of building godly character in your children. This kind of parent is the type of parent God can use to manage His church.

Jesus Is Our Example for Stewarding Our Families

Jesus is the perfect bridegroom. He loves His bride, the church, so much that He gave Himself up for her so that *she might be holy and without blemish* (Ephesians 5:25-27).

Jesus also displayed perfection in His familial relationships. He was the perfect human child (see Hebrews 5:9). He became strong, was filled with wisdom, and experienced the favor of God (Luke 2:40). He was the perfect adult son, making provisions for His mom even while He hung on the cross (John 19:26-27)! He demonstrated perfection as God's Son, knowing at the age of twelve that He must be about His Father's business (Luke 2:49). As God's Son, He learned obedience through what He suffered in His human experience (Hebrews 5:8).

Jesus is also the perfect father – not to be confused with His and our heavenly Father. Rather, Jesus is the *Everlasting Father* (Isaiah 9:6), or the benevolent protector, which is the role that kings fulfilled to care for their people (Isaiah 22:21). As our Everlasting Father, Jesus' care and provision over us will never cease. Amen.

Chapter 4

Be Trustworthy

If you had to choose, would you rather hire someone who is skilled in his or her position or someone who is trustworthy? A presenter posed this question at a pastor's conference I (J. J.) once attended. Those in attendance unanimously agreed that they would rather hire a trustworthy person. Skills can be acquired, but a lack of trustworthiness says something about the person's character.

Paul's qualifications for leadership in his letters to Timothy and Titus insinuate trustworthiness (leaders must be self-controlled, respectable, upright, and not greedy for dishonest gain), but Paul specifically addresses the character trait in 2 Timothy 2:2 when he explains who is worthy to advance the gospel: *What you have heard from me in the presence of many witnesses entrust to faithful men, who will be able to teach others also.* For the gospel to be preserved for future generations, it would need to be in the hands of those who were faithful (Greek: *pistos* – faithful, true, trustworthy) and competent.

When Jethro observed that his son-in-law, Moses, carried the sole burden of judging the Israelites, Jethro told Moses to delegate the responsibilities, but not just to anyone. He said, *Look for able men from all the people, men who fear God, who are trustworthy and hate a bribe* (Exodus 18:21). Jethro knew that those in positions of leadership must be godly men with good morals. If not, they could not be counted on to faithfully execute their responsibilities.

The church needs to be led by dependable and honest people who can be examples of godliness and purity. Following are several ways to develop trustworthiness in your life and ministry so that you, too, can be entrusted with the gospel.

1. Be Reliable

Reliability is one of the hallmarks of trustworthiness. If you are unreliable, others will not trust you. People want to follow leaders they can rely on. To be such a leader:

1. Keep your word. Always deliver on your promises and commitments. It is disheartening to others when you cancel appointments at the last minute or when you don't do what you said you were going to do.

2. Keep a schedule. Don't rely on your memory to keep track of appointments or meetings. Record your obligations in a day planner or schedule-keeping app.

3. Use daily to-do lists. Keep a list of all your

responsibilities, even the ones that aren't appealing to you. Be aware of your responsibilities that need to be filled, and learn to find the joy in completing a task and being able to cross it off your to-do list.

4. Be punctual. Arrive at events, meetings, and appointments early. Use the adage: Early is on time, on time is late, and late is unacceptable. Being punctual speaks volumes about your character. It says that you respect others and their time.

The members of your church are not the only ones who will benefit from your reliability. Your friends need someone they can depend on. Your spouse needs a reliable partner. Your children need a mom and dad who keep their promises. Reliability strengthens all of our relationships.

2. Be Honest

In Billy Joel's hit "Honesty," he sings, "Honesty is such a lonely word. Everyone is so untrue." He isn't too far off with his claim. We all have issues at times with telling the truth. There are plenty of reasons for this gap in our integrity. We lie:

- to shirk our responsibilities (e.g., calling in sick for work)

- to get what we want

- to get ahead (e.g., cheating on taxes)

- to avoid getting in trouble

- to protect others' feelings

- to hide parts of our lives we don't want others to see

- to cover up lies we've told

Your sin nature will always try to tempt you to tell a lie in order to protect yourself from negative consequences. This only compounds the problem. First, whatever you lied about does not go away. Second, when the truth comes out – and it will come out – you still have to face the original problem you lied about. Third, you will now be viewed as a liar.

Believers in Christ are commanded not to lie (Colossians 3:9). God delights in truth (Psalm 51:6). These are reasons enough to be honest with others, but there are practical reasons as well. For example, you will lose credibility with those you lead if you're dishonest.

To cultivate honesty in your life:

1. Resolve to be a person of integrity. Make a promise to yourself that you will tell the truth no matter the consequences. A person of integrity is willing to face the consequences that lying would avoid.

2. Pay attention to the times you plan to lie to cover up the truth. Many lies are conceived before they are uttered. When you think about a troubling situation in which you are at fault, you may consider concocting a lie to protect yourself. Take these thoughts captive and make them obedient to Christ (2 Corinthians 10:5). Plan to tell the truth.

3. Ask God to purge deceit from your heart. David

asked God to search his heart to see if there was anything grievous or deceitful within him (Psalm 139:23-24). If you ask God to help you reveal areas of deceit, He will.

3. Honor Confidentiality

If someone tells you something in confidence, are you tempted to share it with someone else? (e.g., "Keep this between me and you, but . . ."). You will lose others' trust if you do not honor what they tell you in private. People in your church confide in you because they trust you.

To be a person who others trust with their secrets, commit to practicing the Golden Rule. Jesus said, *So whatever you wish that others would do to you, do also to them* (Matthew 7:12). You wouldn't want someone to disclose something you said in confidence, so keep the Golden Rule in mind when you're tempted to betray a confidence.

Train yourself to derive pleasure from keeping information to yourself. It feels good to be trustworthy.

If you do disclose someone's secret, humbly apologize to that person immediately, confessing that you have violated his or her trust. Your humility and honesty will, hopefully, help you salvage the trustworthiness you lost by betraying the person's confidence.

4. Continue to Learn and Grow

To be a trustworthy leader, people need to trust that you are capable of doing your job. That's why Paul told

Timothy to entrust the gospel to faithful men who are able to teach (2 Timothy 2:2). Trustworthiness is more than having integrity. It also signifies competence.[12] Your doctor may be honest, but you also want him to be competent if you are to trust him. The people in your church need to know you have competence in your area of ministry if they are to trust you. "Honest people who are incompetent in their professed area of expertise are not trustworthy."[13]

We've emphasized in this book that character trumps skills, but that's not to say that skill building is unimportant. We've focused on the truth that your skills are meaningless if your thoughts, attitudes, words, and actions are displeasing to God. But by all means, continue to gain and improve skills in your area of expertise. You must display ministerial and leadership competence and be able to cast vision, set and achieve goals, solve problems, and lead effectively if others are to place their trust in you as their leader.

Are you a trustworthy leader? If you cultivate this crucial character trait, you will be in a position of sustained influence. You will have the respect and loyalty of those you lead, and even more importantly, you will prove that you have the character to be a steward of God's household.

---

12   Stephen Covey, *Principle-Centered Leadership* (New York: Free Press, 1991), 171.

13   Covey, *Leadership*, 171.

Jesus Is Our Model for Trustworthiness

It is comforting to know that Jesus is trustworthy in all He says and does. One of His names is *Faithful and True* (Revelation 19:11), which embodies His character.

Jesus told His followers many things, and every word that flowed from His mouth exuded truth. He told a government official that his dying son would be well, and his son was healed (John 4:46-54). He told Peter that he would deny Him three times, and Peter did (Matthew 26:69-75). He told His disciples that although He was leaving them, He would not leave them as orphans (John 14:18), and they received the indwelling of the Holy Spirit (Acts 2:4).

Every time Jesus made a promise, it became a reality. He is trustworthy, and we can have complete trust in His words and actions. What an example to follow! As you resolve to be faithful and true, put your faith in Christ to form you into His likeness.

Chapter 5

Be Disciplined

When I (J. J.) served as a minister of music, I became friends with the church's youth pastor. He connected well with the teens, and his future in ministry looked very promising. He had charisma and a heart to see the lost won to Christ. However, he had a major flaw that the senior pastor was unable to overlook: he was late to just about everything. He showed up to our morning staff meetings and weekend worship services both late and tired.

As his friend, I knew why he was consistently tardy. He stayed up late every night playing video games. It was not unusual for him to play until three or four a.m., leaving him lethargic and unable to meet his time commitments. He put his passion (or addiction) for playing video games ahead of his ministry. After receiving multiple warnings, the youth pastor was fired. He could have been a great leader if he had paid attention to his character.

Before you can govern others, you must be able to govern yourself. You will be unable to govern yourself, however, without discipline. A disciplined person exerts self-control. He might enjoy playing video games, but he doesn't let that or any other activity dominate him. Paul wrote, *"All things are lawful for me," but I will not be dominated by anything* (1 Corinthians 6:12). The disciplined leader is in charge of his moods, appetites, passions, and actions.

Paul requires church leaders to be disciplined (1 Timothy 1:2; Titus 1:8), a character trait he modeled throughout his ministry. He told the Corinthians that he disciplined himself so that he could be effective in his gospel mission: *Every athlete exercises self-control in all things. . . . I discipline my body and keep it under control, lest after preaching to others I myself should be disqualified* (1 Corinthians 9:25, 27).

A serious athlete undergoes intense physical training in order to reach optimal performance. Such an athlete trains when he doesn't feel like it, avoids unhealthy foods when he craves them, and makes numerous sacrifices so he can defeat the competition. To become disciplined, you must exert the will to say no when a forceful appetite inside screams yes. The following will help you build discipline in your life so you will not be disqualified to lead others.

1. Honor Your Commitments

Discipline is the ability to keep promises and to honor commitments. As a starting point, begin making "small" promises to yourself. If you start small and fulfill small promises, you will gradually build your sense of personal honor and your capacity to keep large promises.[14]

A small promise, albeit a consequential one, we can make to ourselves is to get out of bed early. Disciplined people resolve to arise at a specific time. They win the battle of mind over mattress. If you let the mattress win, a chain of unhappy events follows: You find yourself getting up late, then beginning a frantic rush to get dressed, organized, fed, and out of the house. In the rush, you grow impatient and insensitive to others. Nerves get frayed and tempers are short – and all because of sleeping in.[15]

What is the result of honoring your commitment to get up early? You begin your morning with a private victory. This gives you a sense of conquering, which propels you to conquer challenges all day long. Success breeds success. To win the battle of mind over mattress and cultivate discipline, promise to get up at a certain time every morning, regardless if you feel like it or not. Next, promise to use that first hour in a profitable way, preparing for the day. Then carry out your plan.[16] By doing this, you will have the momentum to take charge of your life.

2. Steward Your Time Wisely

In his classic book *Spiritual Leadership,* Oswald Sanders

---

14   Stephen Covey, *Principle-Centered Leadership* (New York: Free Press, 1991), 73.

15   Covey, *Leadership*, 51.

16   Covey, Leadership, 73.

says that for a leader to become effective, he or she must overcome "slothful habits." An effective church leader will "work while others waste time, study while others snooze, pray while others daydream."[17]

The best way to conquer laziness and procrastination is to create a schedule and adhere to it. Without a schedule, you'll be tempted to let your feelings determine your actions:

> "I'm not in the mood to meet with Tim today. I think I'll postpone it."

> "I'm not motivated to work on my sermon this morning."

> "I don't feel like praying."

> "I'll do that task later."

Disciplined people don't submit to their feelings, moods, or circumstances. Their schedule is their servant, and they exercise discipline to organize weekly and adapt daily. They schedule blocks of time for their work and stay committed to their schedules.[18]

Do not attempt to be in a leadership position at your church without a daily calendar. You need one to track your appointments and to schedule time for tasks on your to-do list. Get into the habit of planning tomorrow's schedule today. Such discipline will increase your fruitfulness.

---

17 Oswald Sanders, *Spiritual Leadership* (Chicago: Moody Publishers, 2007), 61.

18 Covey, *Leadership*, 73.

3. Train Yourself to Be Godly

Paul said, *Train yourself for godliness; for while bodily training is of some value, godliness is of value in every way, as it holds promise for the present life and also for the life to come* (1 Timothy 4:7-8). A significant part of your training for godliness includes a consistent time in God's Word, a planned time for reading, and meditation. If you're too busy to not have a consistent daily time of prayer and devotion, your priorities need to be reevaluated right now. Your church does not need a leader who fails to discipline himself for godliness.

Commit to a set time every day to study God's Word and pray. If you're a pastor and have preaching responsibilities, many of your sermon ideas will arise during your devotional times. But don't allow your quiet time to simply become your sermon prep time. In other words, when you're sermonizing, your focus is on what you're giving: a sermon. When you have a time of devotion, keep your focus on what you're receiving from God to make you Christlike.

Some choose to begin their day with God. My coauthor, B. W., disciplines himself to wake up at 4:30 a.m. After he makes coffee, he invests an hour to read, study, and meditate on the Greek New Testament. He likes reading in Greek during his devotions because it forces him to read slowly. He reads God's Word at other times during the day, but he starts the day with God's Word (and a strong cup of joe). His goal is godliness. We grow in godliness when we have a planned time to study Scripture and apply it to our lives.

4. Maintain Your Health

Disciplined people eat healthy foods, get adequate rest, and exercise regularly. The quality of our personal lives and our work is adversely affected when we allow ourselves to overeat, stay up late, or not exercise.[19] Make a promise to yourself to take good care of your body. While training for godliness is valuable in every way, "bodily training is of some value" (1 Timothy 4:8). John Piper has experienced the "some value" principle throughout his long ministerial career. He lifts weights and jogs three times per week, disciplining himself to exercise for the glory of God. His words are inspiring:

> In short, I have one life to live for Jesus (2 Cor. 5:15). I don't want to waste it. My approach is not to lengthen it but to maximize purity and productivity now. I want to show as much gospel truth and publish as much gospel truth as I can. I have found, for forty-four years, that exercise helps.[20]

B. W. and I also apply the "some value" principle to our lives. At ages 55 and 56 (I'm the senior), we exercise five days per week and play basketball as often as we can.

Exercise will help you as well, and so will a healthy diet. Making wise food choices is foundational to taking care of your body, God's temple (1 Corinthians 3:16; 6:19).

---

19   Covey, *Leadership*, 50.
20   John Piper, *Brothers, We Are Not Professionals* (Nashville: B&H Publishing 2013), 187.

Skip the junk food and fast food and opt for nutritional choices that will give you energy and good health.

5. Commit to Sexual Purity

Paul said that he disciplines his body to *keep it under control* (1 Corinthians 9:27), which most likely refers to sexual sin, since sexual immorality disqualifies anyone from preaching and leading the church.[21] If you struggle with pornography or sexual immorality of any kind, get help immediately. Don't let this secret sin reign in your life and rule it. The church needs leaders who walk in fidelity and sexual purity.

There is a reason Paul includes discipline on his list of qualifications for church leaders. Disciplined people resist inside forces (e.g., moods, feelings) and outside factors (circumstances and situations) so they can do the work God has called them to do. They're in charge of their attitudes and actions, not swayed by their emotions or appetites. As you continue to grow in discipline, start today by making small promises to yourself, and keeping them.

Jesus Is Our Model of Discipline

It takes spiritual discipline and self-control to endure the challenges and tragedies that befall us in this life, especially if we have the power or resources to easily get out of them.

---

21   John MacArthur, *One Faithful Life: A Harmony of the Life and Writings of the Apostle Paul* (Nashville: Thomas Nelson, 2019), 174.

There are many times Jesus could have used His divine authority and power to His advantage. He could have called down twelve legions of angels to protect Him from being arrested, but He went along peacefully (Matthew 26:53). He could have smitten the soldiers who stripped Him, spit on Him, struck Him, and crowned Him with thorns, but He remained silent (Matthew 27:27-31). He could have come down from the humiliating cross, but because of His disciplined obedience to God's eternal plan, He died on the tree, forsaken by all (Matthew 27:45-50).

We may not have the discipline and self-control to maintain perfect devotion and obedience to God like Jesus did, but in Him we have a perfect example to follow when trials come and we want to take the easy way out. As you resolve to be a disciplined and self-controlled leader, put your faith in Christ to make you more and more like Him. He will help you become disciplined in every area of your life.

Chapter 6

Be Upright

It is essential for leaders to be upright. The Greek word for upright is *dikaios*, which means righteous and just. There are two ways this word is used in the Bible. First, a believer becomes *dikaios* the minute he or she is saved. Second, *dikaios* describes how a believer should live. Leaders who are rich in *dikaios* are impartial and fair. They make decisions initiated by love, and they are peacemakers. James tells us that the prayers of a *dikaios* person are powerful and effective (James 5:16). Upon Jesus' death, a Roman centurion declared, *Certainly this man was* dikaios (Luke 23:47).

When people know that their leader is upright, they feel emotionally safe, and they know they will always be treated with fairness and respect. To develop this trait in your life, four actions are necessary.

1. Be Impartial

James is very clear: *My brothers, show no partiality as you hold the faith in our Lord Jesus Christ* (James 2:1). He tells us that when we show favoritism by treating some people better than others, we make ourselves *judges with evil thoughts* (James 2:4).

It is easy to be partial to people who can benefit us or our church. We might justify our partiality by saying, "Hey, I'm only scratching their backs because they scratch mine. Besides, it's for the good of the church and for the good of God's kingdom." But in reality, we are viewing truth through a distorted lens in order to justify our favoritism. James shattered that distorted lens when he said, *If you show partiality, you are committing sin and are convicted by the law as transgressors* (James 2:9).

God shows no partiality, and neither do upright leaders. I (B. W.) once worked for a boss whom I'll call "Mr. N," who was quite partial. There were several staff members whom Mr. N. favored over everyone else, and he had no qualms about showing it. This character flaw led to some big problems in the organization. Within months of Mr. N.'s arrival, the staff's once symbiotic chemistry changed drastically. Staff members began competing against one another as they sought inclusion in Mr. N.'s inner circle. The competition often got ugly. Gossip, backstabbing, and even false accusations became all too common. Shockingly, Mr. N. reveled in this toxic situation. After he moved on to a new organization, our new boss had to spend many months undoing the damage caused by Mr. N.'s partiality.

Partiality breaks Christ's *royal law* of love: *You shall*

love your neighbor as yourself (James 2:8; Matthew 22:39). Such love means seeking the highest good of others. Partiality is seeking only the desires and interests of the one who is playing favorites. If we are serious about fulfilling the law of Christ, we must treat every brother and sister in the household of God equally.

2. Be Fair

Fairness is a hallmark of the upright leader. Solomon told us in Ecclesiastes that life is not inherently fair. The race does not always go to the fastest, nor the battle to the strongest (Ecclesiastes 9:11), but the upright leader strives to show fairness in all things under his or her influence. In fact, God demands it: *The Lord demands accurate scales and balances; he sets the standards for fairness* (Proverbs 16:11 NLT).

When Jesus said, *Whatever you wish that others would do to you, do also to them* (Matthew 7:12), He was prescribing fairness. Most people do not notice unfairness when it happens to others, but notice immediately if it happens to them. The Golden Rule is an excellent blueprint for fairness. Always ask yourself: Is this how I would want to be treated?

3. Make Just Decisions

Leaders make dozens of decisions every day. Most of them are relatively minor, such as, "What refreshments should I put out for the meeting?" But some are of much greater magnitude, even life-changing, such as, "Do I need to move this staff member from full-time to part-time?"

Upright leaders seek God's wisdom when making decisions. Every decision has its own unique specifics, but the following four steps are always important.

1. **Pray for wisdom.** By not seeking God's wisdom, you take leadership decisions in your own hands. There are many biblical examples of upright men seeking God's guidance prior to taking any action. For example, when King Jehoshaphat discovered that a vast army was coming against him and the people of Judah, they faced a tough decision and began with prayer: *We do not know what to do, but our eyes are on you* (2 Chronicles 20:12).

   James offers an important reminder for leaders facing a difficult decision: *If any of you lacks wisdom, let him ask God, who gives generously without reproach, and it will be given him* (James 1:5). Proverbs tells us that the Lord has a treasure of wisdom waiting for us: *He stores up sound wisdom for the upright* (Proverbs 2:7).

2. **Seek godly counsel.** If you are to be effective at home, at church, or at work, you need the godly counsel of others. If you continually act in your own wisdom and understanding, you will be blinded by your feelings, bias, and impressions. Every wise leader is open to godly advice. King Solomon said, *The way of the fool is right in his own eyes, but a wise man listens to advice* (Proverbs 12:15).

   The consequences can be devastating for leaders who do not seek advice, but rewarding for leaders who do: *Where there is no guidance, a people falls, but in abundance of counselors there is safety* (Proverbs 11:14). Do not seek advice from just anyone, however; be sure to have godly counselors in your life. These individuals will help you expand your alternatives and evaluate your decisions.

3. **Seek God's Word.** God's Word is a lamp to guide our feet and a light for our path (Psalm 119:105). We can count on God's Word as instructions for making decisions in all areas of our lives because the Bible gives us truth concerning relationships, upright living, business matters, and even investments!

   The Bible also gives us truth concerning matters related to church ministry and leadership. First, we need to seek to ensure that our decisions are aligned with biblical principles. Whenever you face a decision, consult God's Word. He will guide you with His counsel (Psalm 73:24).

4. **Look to glorify God.** As believers who are called to glorify God in all we do and say (1 Corinthians 10:31), a question we should ask before making any decision is, "Does this decision glorify God?" If you're not sure that the answer is yes, you need to check your motives for making the decision. If your decision or its impact is self-serving and does not honor and glorify God, it needs to be scrapped.

   Upright leaders make just decisions because their decisions are rooted in prayer, godly counsel, God's Word, and a desire to give God glory.

4. Be a Peacemaker

Upright leaders pursue both personal and social justice. They seek conflict resolution at a personal level as they seek reconciliation in whatever context they live and work.[22]

You will face both personal and churchwide conflict. Count on it. Personal conflict arises when church members disapprove of what you've said or done or come against you because of a decision you've made. Churchwide conflict comes when people take sides on an issue, and it can be as devastating as a church split. Upright leaders will immediately address anyone or anything that threatens unity in the Christian community.

In *The Peacemaker: A Biblical Guide to Resolving Personal Conflict*, Ken Sande presents four biblical steps for conflict resolution.[23] Follow these steps at home and at church whenever peace and harmony is threatened.

Step 1: Glorify God
Every conflict is an opportunity to honor God. Paul said, *So, whether you eat or drink, or whatever you do, do all to the glory of God* (1 Corinthians 10:31). When we intentionally choose to give God glory as we approach the conflict resolution process, our perspective changes. Our goal is no longer just to resolve conflict but to magnify God's greatness and His grace, mercy, and love. Following are ways to glorify God in the midst of a conflict.

---

22   William Mounce, "Biblical Leadership in the Pastoral Epistles," p. 9. Accessed October 5, 2021. www.biblicaltraining.org.

23   Ken Sande, *The Peacemaker* (Grand Rapids: Baker Books, 2004).

1. **Trust Him.** Trust God to show you how to resolve the conflict, leaning not on your own understanding but on His wisdom (Proverbs 3:5-7). Trust involves a deep reliance on God and confidence in His promise that *all things work together for good* for those who love God and *are called according to his purpose* (Romans 8:28).

2. **Obey Him.** God calls us to walk in unity and love with one another, *standing firm in one spirit, with one mind striving side by side for the faith of the gospel* (Philippians 1:27). Be obedient when the Holy Spirit leads you to build brotherly affection and harmony. By doing so, your love for others will abound more and more, *to the glory and praise of God* (Philippians 1:11).

3. **Imitate Him.** Anyone who abides in Christ will *walk in the same way in which [Christ] walked* (1 John 2:6). Imitating God means mirroring His humility, mercy, forgiveness, and love.

4. **Acknowledge Him.** When reconciliation takes place, this is a gospel moment. Use it to give God praise and glory for being the architect of the reconciliation process. As others acknowledge you for being able to respond to conflict in effective ways, tell them it is God who has been working in you to do the things you could never accomplish on your own (Philippians 2:13; 1 Peter 3:14-16).[24]

---

24   Sande, *Peacemaker*, 31-33.

As you pursue conflict resolution, above all else, seek to honor and glorify God.

Step 2: Get the Log Out of Your Eye

We must not ignore our own faults as we call the faults of others into question. Jesus said:

> *Why do you see the speck that is in your brother's eye, but you do not notice the log that is in your own eye? Or how can you say to your brother, "Let me take the speck out of your eye," when there is the log in your own eye? You hypocrite, first take the log out of your own eye, and then you will see clearly to take the speck out of your brother's eye.* (Matthew 7:3-5)

Biblical peacemaking is not possible without log removal. We must take ownership of our own contributions to a conflict before we can focus on what others have done. We must also ask if the offense can be overlooked. Where love abounds, so does grace. Peter said, *Above all, keep loving one another earnestly, since love covers a multitude of sins* (1 Peter 4:8).

After you have taken a thorough inventory of your own role in the conflict and you have decided that the conflict cannot be overlooked, you are ready for the next step.

Step 3: Gently Restore

Paul wrote, *Brothers, if anyone is caught in any*

transgression, you who are spiritual should restore him in a spirit of gentleness (Galatians 6:1). In Step 2 you analyze your role in the conflict, and in Step 3 you lovingly let the person know their role. If others fail to see their contributions to a conflict, we need to graciously show them their fault.[25]

Oftentimes your humble confession will be followed by one of his or her own. This is called the Golden Result. While the Golden Rule calls us to do unto others as we would have them do unto us, the Golden Result says that people will usually treat us the way we treat them. If we sincerely tell someone, "I was wrong," he or she will often say, "It was my fault, too."[26]

If you confess your fault to the other person, but he or she responds negatively or offers a superficial confession, you have several options:

1. Overlook the offense (1 Peter 4:8).

2. Build on the superficial confession with segments such as, "I appreciate your words. May I further explain my frustration?"

3. Involve church leaders or respected believers who can help encourage repentance (Matthew 18:16).

4. Postpone the confrontation for another time.

If the other person is responsible, you can rejoice that God is glorified through the conflict. It's time to forgive as God forgives (see Ephesians 4:32 and Colossians 3:13).

---

25   Sande, *Peacemaker*, 12-13.

26   Sande, *Peacemaker*, 78.

Step 4: Go and Be Reconciled

The final step to peacemaking involves a commitment to restoring damaged relationships. Jesus put reconciliation above offering gifts at the altar. He said, *First be reconciled to your brother, and then come and offer your gift* (Matthew 5:24).

When you truly forgive someone, it means that you release the other person from all debts concerning the conflict. He or she is released from your punishments, grudges, and resentment. Sande says that when we forgive others as Jesus has forgiven, "the debris of conflict is cleared away and the door is opened for genuine peace."[27]

As you apply these biblical peacemaking steps to your life and ministry, you will create a culture of peace in both your home and church. You will stop seeing disputes and disagreements as obstacles and start seeing them as opportunities to glorify God.

The church is in desperate need of upright leaders who lead with impartiality, fairness, a commitment to make godly decisions, and a heart for life-changing reconciliation. Be that leader.

Jesus Is our Model of Uprightness

Paul told Timothy that church leaders must be *dikaios*. This is commonly translated into English as "upright," but it has a range of meanings. *Dikaios* can be translated upright, righteous, just, or innocent. Jesus is all of these.

---

27   Sande, *Peacemaker*, 13.

Jesus is upright. He treated everyone in an upright manner. His disciples were shocked that He would associate with a Samaritan woman (John 4:9). The Pharisees marveled that He socialized with sinners and tax collectors (Matthew 9:10-13). Yet He was the same person no matter who He was with. He never played favorites.

Jesus is righteous. He is the perfect lamb *without blemish or spot* (1 Peter 1:19). When Paul reminds us that *none is righteous, no, not one* (Romans 3:10), he is correct. We will never be righteous on our own. We need to rely on the one who is: Jesus. Any righteousness we have is through Him.

Jesus is just. When He was confronted with a woman caught in adultery, Jesus shined a light on a great injustice of the Pharisees – the desire to execute punishment for a capital sin while they were all guilty of capital sins themselves. His impromptu lesson on justice caused them to retract their charges and abandon the situation. Being just also means opposing that which is unjust.

Jesus is innocent. In Luke's account of Jesus' death, Luke quotes a Roman centurion who declared Jesus *dikaios*. Some Bible versions translate *dikaios* in this case as "righteous," while others choose "innocent." Clearly both are accurate given what we know about Jesus. It is more appropriate to use "innocent" in this context because the penalty of crucifixion was commonly handed down based on *guilt*. We know Pontius

Pilate declared Jesus *without guilt* several times. An upright leader should be above reproach so that he will always be judged "without reproach."

Clearly Jesus is upright, righteous, just, and innocent. This begs the question: Are you and I? According to Paul, leaders who aren't *dikaios* have no business leading others.

Chapter 7

Be Gentle

There was a well-known Christian leader who was once on top of the world. His growing megachurch of fourteen thousand regular attenders influenced a whole movement of church plants, and his sermon podcasts dominated download charts. Thousands flocked to his conferences.

Many were shocked when he was asked to resign from the church he had founded. He wasn't asked to resign because of sexual immorality or financial improprieties. Instead, he had just fired two elders who disagreed with him. He shamed them publicly and asked all church members to shun them. This was the straw that broke the camel's back.

As it turns out, the pastor unleashed his anger quite regularly on his staff and elders. Several of his staff members who were worn down by his continual abrasiveness and harshness called for him to step down. In his official resignation letter to the church, he confessed and repented of pride, anger, and a domineering spirit.

The church disbanded its centralized operations, and the leader took some time away from public ministry to develop his character. Today he is a pastor who continues to publish books and make contributions to biblical and ministerial thought. We pray that he has made character changes so he can successfully lead God's church, and hopefully those around him get to see a kinder and gentler Christian leader.

Paul disqualifies anyone from leadership who is not gentle (1 Timothy 3:3; Titus 1:7). Those who are violent and quick-tempered do not demonstrate a life that is led and guided by the Holy Spirit. They don't demonstrate lives that are joined to Christ's life (John 15:4-5). When we live according to the Spirit, He produces Christ's character in us. We are gentle because Christ is gentle. Jesus said, *Learn from me, for I am gentle and lowly in heart* (Matthew 11:29).

Jesus displayed gentleness whenever He interacted with others. He didn't harshly rebuke the woman at the well for her adulterous lifestyle (John 4:7-26). With gentleness and compassion, He revealed her sin and His knowledge of her life. Jesus showed compassion to the woman caught in adultery. The religious leaders wanted to stone her, but Jesus defended her, saying that only a sinless person could throw the first stone. Rather than condemning her, He gently said, *Go, and from now on sin no more* (John 8:2-11).

Throughout the gospels, we discover a gentle Jesus, and Jesus wants us to learn from Him. Some Christian leaders, however, are slow learners. They are harsh with their staff or volunteer workers, and they're quick to rebuke those who disagree with them. Oswald Sanders wrote, "If you would rather pick a fight than solve a problem, do not consider leading the church."[28] Gentle leaders always seek peaceful solutions and are able to diffuse explosive situations.

The church needs leaders who speak the truth but do so in love (Ephesians 4:15). The church needs gentle leaders. Following are several biblical principles to put into practice as you seek to display gentleness.

1. Speak Calmly When Others Are Angry

King Solomon said, *A soft answer turns away wrath, but a harsh word stirs up anger* (Proverbs 15:1). When someone is upset with you and speaks curtly to you, don't return his or her harsh words with some of your own. Yes, this can be easier said than done, but as you allow the Holy Spirit to work in your life, overcome your instinct to react. Instead, be gracious and respond to anger with a gentle voice, a humble spirit, and a relaxed posture.

Picture the scene: Jesus and His disciples are on the Sea of Galilee when a fierce storm arises. Fearing that their lives are in jeopardy, the disciples are upset with Jesus, for although they are all about to die, He is asleep in the stern. They wake Him up and plead, *Teacher, do you not care that we are perishing?* (Mark 4:38). He cares. He also cares about their lack of faith, but He doesn't scold them or put them in their place. He speaks

---

28 Oswald Sanders, *Spiritual Leadership* (Chicago: Moody Publishers, 2007), 48.

to them with words that are calm and steady: *Why are you afraid, O you of little faith?* (Matthew 8:26). Then Jesus miraculously calms the storm. Jesus models self-control, speaking to His frantic disciples with calmness and composure.

2. Correct Others with Love

Paul tells Timothy that *the Lord's servant must not be quarrelsome but kind to everyone, . . . correcting his opponents with gentleness* (2 Timothy 2:24-25). Paul modeled such behavior when he brought correction to the Corinthians. A rebellious minority, influenced by Paul's opponents, had rejected the gospel and Paul's apostolic ministry. Paul's love and kindness are clearly seen in his words to this minority: *I Paul, myself entreat you, by the meekness and gentleness of Christ* (2 Corinthians 10:1). Then in 2 Corinthians 10 through 14, Paul corrected his opponents, but even in his boldness he exuded the love of Christ. He wrote, *It is in the sight of God that we have been speaking in Christ, and all for your upbuilding, beloved* (2 Corinthians 12:19).

Speaking the truth in love (Ephesians 4:15) is the approach Christian leaders are to take whenever correction is necessary. Before you correct anyone, make sure that your concern for their spiritual well-being is what's motivating you. If it is, ask God to help you speak to the person with the meekness and gentleness of Christ.

3. Restore Backslidden Believers
with Gentleness

When Jesus appeared to His disciples after His resurrection, He restored Peter with gentleness. Some people in Jesus' shoes (or sandals) might have hunted Peter down and rebuked him for his thrice denial. Not Jesus. He said, *Simon, son of John, do you love me more than these?* (John 21:15). Jesus gave Peter an opportunity to declare his loyalty and love for Him.

When those in your church (or house) sin or fall away from God, it may be tempting in your frustration to come down on them with strong, condemning words. You may even be tempted to abandon them. We know people who committed felonies who were abandoned by the leaders of their church as soon as they were arrested. Rather than showering them with God's redemptive grace, these leaders wanted nothing to do with the errant believers. Paul said, *If anyone is caught in any transgression, you who are spiritual should restore him in a spirit of gentleness.* And you should be careful, too, Paul added, *lest you too be tempted* (Galatians 6:1).

Every believer is eligible for restoration. If Jesus could restore Peter, who denied that he even knew Jesus, then you and I can gently restore those who are caught in sin. As you do, you'll be demonstrating that Christ's character is being developed in you.

4. Defend the Gospel with Gentleness

You will occasionally encounter atheists and those who

oppose the gospel. These discussions can be fruitful. Paul often reasoned with Jews, trying to persuade them that Jesus was the Messiah. Some of the Jews were convinced and even joined Paul in his ministry, along with some devout Greeks and prominent women (Acts 17:2-4).

Some people use aggressive tactics when sharing their faith amid opposition. They'll try to prove they're right, often belittling the person with whom they are arguing. For example, a person might say, "How can any intelligent person believe that we evolved from monkeys? I thought you were smarter than that!" Defending the gospel does not mean attacking the person. This is bad apologetics. We are called to present and defend the gospel with love. *Always [be] prepared to make a defense to anyone who asks you for a reason for the hope that is in you; yet do it with gentleness and respect* (1 Peter 3:15). The result? Others will see Christ's love and meekness in you, and this example will be more powerful than any argument you might present.

As you cultivate Christ's character in your life and ministry, let your gentleness be evident to everyone (Philippians 4:5). But if you're rude or abrasive, you give no evidence of Christ's power and presence in your life. Submit to the will of the Holy Spirit and to the lordship of Christ. You will become more large-hearted and considerate, and your gentle spirit will be on full display as an example for others to follow.

Jesus Is Our Model of Gentleness

Kind. Tenderhearted. Loving in all His ways. Jesus is

the perfect example of gentleness. *Hold on a second,* you may be thinking, *what about when Jesus overturned the tables of the money changers?* Even in His anger, Jesus was in control of his emotions. When you have a submissive spirit like Christ, even your anger is controlled and directed only towards sin. This is called righteous indignation.

When the merchants of the temple tried to profit from people's desire to be made right with God, Jesus displayed anger and overturned the tables of the merchants and the seats of those who sold pigeons (Matthew 21:12). But in His anger, He did not sin. He wasn't rude. He didn't speak harshly. He did, however, come against that which was wrong. Then He addressed their wrongdoing with correction: *"My house shall be called a house of prayer,"* but you make it a den of robbers (Matthew 21:13).

Being gentle doesn't mean that you're never angry. It doesn't mean that you have to be passive. It doesn't mean you're a pushover. It does mean that you speak to others in a way that reveals that Christ is in you, working to make you more like Him. Without a spirit of gentleness, you'll be prone to sin in your anger, which will give the devil an opportunity to sow discord (Ephesians 4:26-27).

Gentleness is a key requirement for Christian leaders (1 Timothy 3:3). Invite the Holy Spirit to help you display Christ's character as you become a leader who demonstrates gentleness, even amid anger.

Chapter 8

Be Hospitable

Have you ever been in a person's house and felt less than welcomed? You aren't offered a seat or something to drink, and the host has an air of impatience. It almost feels like he or she is anxious for you to be on your way. This is the opposite of how Christians, especially Christian leaders, are to behave. We are to live the gospel through hospitality and deeds of kindness. Timothy Keller wrote, "Hospitality done well is generous, uncomplaining, loving, and refreshing. It does not make guests feel like 'guests' but like members of a family. Hospitality provides a feeling of security, warmth, safety, and love."[29]

Jesus gives us the standard for hospitality: *For I was hungry and you gave me food, I was thirsty and you gave me drink, I was a stranger and you welcomed me, I was naked and you clothed me, I was sick and you visited me, I was in prison and you came to me* (Matthew 25:35-36).

---

29   Timothy Keller, *Gospel in Life Study Guide* (Grand Rapids: Zondervan, 2010), 78.

Jesus' words describe the acts of kindness we can do every day. When we choose to do so, we are not only showing biblical hospitality to a brother or sister, but we are showing it to Christ Himself.

Paul requires Christian leaders to be hospitable (1 Timothy 3:2; Titus 1:8). He holds hospitality in such regard that he even commands Timothy not to take in widows if they have not shown hospitality (1 Timothy 5:10).

Hospitality is one of the fruits of receiving God's grace. Luke exposes this fact in Acts when he tells us of Lydia, a wealthy merchant. In only two verses, we see the Lord's grace and its immediate effect on her. First, God opened Lydia's heart to Him. Second, Lydia opened her heart to others: *The Lord opened her heart to pay attention to what was said by Paul* (Acts 16:14). Lydia then responded by opening her heart and home: *If you have judged me to be faithful to the Lord, come to my house and stay* (Acts 16:15). It is believed that Lydia's home was one of the first church gathering places in Macedonia. Lydia shows us hospitality in action.

Acts 16 is not the last we hear about how grace fuels the hospitality of the Macedonian believers. Paul boasted about them to the church of Corinth when he said, *We want you to know, brothers, about the grace of God that has been given among the churches of Macedonia* (2 Corinthians 8:1). These Macedonian churches were undergoing many afflictions and extreme poverty (v. 2), yet they were *begging . . . earnestly* for the privilege of helping other believers (v. 4). They would surely have opened their homes to share what they had with those in need, but in this case they sent what they had to where the needy believers were.

The examples of Lydia and the Macedonians are two primary ways to show hospitality. Let's look at both.

1. Open Your Home

The Bible tells us to whom we are to open our homes.

We are to open our homes to other Christians. Paul instructs the church to watch for Christians in need and to *seek to show hospitality* (Romans 12:13). He is not describing social entertaining. A person who entertains socially is self-focused, looking to impress others with a spotless home, fancy foods, and symbols of status on full display – all in an effort to shine a spotlight on himself. In contrast, a person showing Christian hospitality is concerned about the guest far more than projecting any status or image.

In Isaiah's day, God's people attempted to flaunt their piety through religious rituals. They went to the temple every day, fasted, and read the Scriptures, but did so for the wrong reasons. In their efforts to elevate themselves, they neglected people around them who were in need. God called His people rebels for their selfish behavior and makes clear what actions He expects when seeking Him sincerely: *Is it not to share your bread with the hungry and bring the homeless poor into your house; when you see the naked, to cover him, and not to hide yourself from your own flesh?* (Isaiah 58:7).

God is more concerned with how we treat others than with how we appear to them. He wants us to show hospitality to our family, Christian leaders, and fellow Christians. It does not require riches, a fancy home, the finest food, or even loads of time. A hospitable host simply has a listening ear and a humble heart and is eager to *contribute to the needs of the saints* (Romans 12:13).

We are to open our homes to missionaries. Sometimes your home can be part of God's plan to spread the gospel. When you open your home to a missionary, you make your home a place of refreshment for those who are on the front lines of worldwide evangelism. You provide rest and renewal, but you also provide financial support. Every meal you prepare, every bed you offer for the night, and every time you lend your vehicle to a missionary allows the missionary to save money on travel and lodging expenses. That money can then be spent in other ways to advance God's kingdom.

Hospitable church leaders provide for itinerant preachers too. Some churches go so far as to buy nearby houses for the sole purpose of hosting itinerant preachers. Jesus makes it clear that these traveling teachers should rightly expect hospitality on their travels (Luke 10:3-9). By opening our homes, we are sons of peace (Luke 10:6).

We are to open our homes to strangers. The author of Hebrews equates showing hospitality to brotherly/sisterly love: *Let brotherly love continue. Do not neglect to show hospitality to strangers, for thereby some have entertained angels unawares. Remember those who are in prison as though in prison with them* (Hebrews 13:1-3). We hold in high regard men and women who reach out and minister to prisoners. Those in this neglected population are not only ignored by Christians but are often despised by them. Showing hospitality to strangers and prisoners can be challenging, but this is what we are called to do.

2. Take Care of Christians Who Are in Need

But if anyone has the world's goods and sees his brother in need, yet closes his heart against him, how does God's love abide in him? (1 John 3:17). John is quite explicit: if you see a believer in need, share your goods. Do not think of it as offering a loan, but think of it as sharing your blessings. Remember, all you have is from heaven (John 3:27).

The Holy Spirit brings unity, and sharing is a natural extension of unity. The members of the early church were so motivated to share that they sold their possessions and shared all they had (see Acts 4:32-37). The result? Nobody among them was in need (Acts 4:34).

Hospitality occurs outside of the home when a person brings or sends his goods to another, yet many churches and individual Christians fail to do this. This failure will come with consequences, for the Bible calls anyone who turns away the needy a transgressor with great sins (Amos 5:12). Why do some believers hesitate to help others or decide not to help those in need? Some common excuses are discussed below.

1. **"My money will be wasted."** God tells us to share what we have. He does not extend to us the authority to put conditions on our gifts to others. Additionally, there are many ways to

help others that do not directly involve cash. We can buy meals, offer new or gently used items, or even better, give our time and effort to serve someone in need.

2. **"The little bit I can offer won't make a difference."** This lazy way of thinking has been around for thousands of years. The thought that an individual cannot affect change is absurd. Indeed, all major endeavors have been accomplished by single entities working in a group, each one seemingly insignificant, yet as a group accomplishing much.

3. **"Scriptural commands to help the poor were intended for people in biblical times."** The call to help others is not confined to a certain time that is now over. Nowhere does God put a time limit on helping others. People who use the "biblical times" excuse do not believe that the Bible is relevant for us today. They don't believe that God's Word is living and active (Hebrews 4:12). God's command to take care of the poor has no expiration date.

4. **"I don't know of anyone in need."** James rebuked Christians for being willfully ignorant of those in need: *If a brother or sister is poorly clothed and lacking in daily food, and one of you says to them, "Go in peace, be warmed and filled," without giving them the things needed for the body, what good is that?* (James 2:15-16). Church leaders must always be aware of those around them in both spiritual and financial need and seek to meet that need.

5. **"I have no time and wouldn't know where to start."** A church leader without time to show hospitality to others has his priorities misplaced. It begins with an "open door" policy. If you prioritize your "work" (sermon writing, planning, budgeting, etc.) over people, you are neglecting your calling. People are your work. Let yourself be interrupted. Open your office just as you would open your home. Always be welcoming to those who pay you a visit at your church – they are your ministry.

The Bible calls us away from individualized, self-centered leadership and woos us to servanthood, in which we are mindful of the needs of those in our churches and attentive to the injustices of the world. As the Holy Spirit works in you to open your heart to God more and more, you will find yourself more and more offering your heart, your home, and your hands to others.

Jesus Is Our Model of Hospitality

Practice hospitality in all of your relationships. You don't have to be close friends with everyone, but you are to be hospitable to those in your house, church, neighborhood, and beyond.

As you grow in Christ's character, let everyone with whom you are in contact see Christ's kindness, generosity, and love in you.

Chapter 9

Be a Lover of Good

Dave is excited about today's church service. It will be his first time to be in charge of the sound system. As lead sound tech, he will engineer the sound for the praise and worship band as well as for the pastor's wireless microphone.

As the band begins, everything sounds great – for about five seconds. Then the unthinkable happens. A high-pitched whine begins to scream from the speakers. One of the many microphones being used feeds back into the amplifiers. Dave's fingers reflect his panic as they fumble across the soundboard, desperately trying to locate and extinguish the ear-stinging squeal. He eventually finds the offending microphone and mutes it. The ordeal only lasts about half a minute, but to Dave it feels like an eternity. With the feedback issue fixed, the rest of the service runs smoothly.

After the closing prayer, Pastor Ward, the worship leader, moves with haste toward the sound booth. He intends to give Dave a harsh reprimand because, in his mind, the entire sound service was ruined. What's worse, Pastor Ward feels like a fool since one of his team members blew it.

Just before Pastor Ward reaches the sound booth, the lead pastor, Pastor Dean, intercepts him. He saw the anger on Pastor Ward's face and took quick action to defuse the situation. The two pastors arrive at the sound booth together. They find Dave standing among the two other sound techs, Dave's face betraying his emotions. He is clearly upset about what happened in the worship service. He feels that he let everyone down. He also thinks he ruined his chance to remain lead sound tech. He even thinks he will be removed from the sound crew altogether. For a moment nobody speaks, and the tension is as thick as dread.

Fortunately, Pastor Dean is a lover of good. He read everyone's body language and facial expressions and went into action. He begins by lightening the mood. With a wide smile he says, "Well, now we know our sound system can really hit those high notes, just like Mariah Carey." Maintaining his playful grin, he gives Dave a wink. He points out to all involved that these things are bound to happen, and while memorable, it was unlikely that thirty seconds of feedback would cost the church many members, if any. "Besides," he says, "I've given plenty of thirty-*minute* sermons that our congregation probably found much more grating on their ears!"

Later, Pastor Dean followed up privately with Pastor Ward, who, after considering the senior pastor's words and putting his pride in check, agreed that a few seconds of noise is not a sign of the end times, let alone a reason to berate a brother.

There is a reason the apostle Paul includes being *a lover of good* in his list of qualifications for being a church leader. It is crucial for every church leader to find the good in every person and in every situation. The phrase *lover of good* (Titus 1:8) comes from a Greek word that combines "friend" (*philos*) with "benevolently good" (*agathos*). One who is *philagathos* is a friend of doing good to others. The person not only does good, but *delights* in doing good. Paul held this character trait in such regard that he reserved the use of *philagathos* for only this occasion. It appears nowhere else in the Bible.

Find the Good in Everyone and Everything

Finding the good in everyone and everything is an essential quality of leadership. It doesn't come naturally. We are prone to criticize, complain, and condemn – so it must be carefully cultivated. Here are five ways to do so.

1. Separate Yourself from the Bad

Paul has much to say about wrong living. He is adamant about how believers should *not* live. As he outlines qualifications for Christian leaders to Titus, he lists many unacceptable behaviors and character traits (see Titus 1:6-16):

- debauchery

- arrogance

- drunkenness

- greed

- laziness

- disobedience

- insubordination

- quick-tempered

- violent

- deceptiveness

- gluttony

Some of the unacceptable behaviors on Paul's list may be easy to avoid because you already don't engage in them. Others, however, may be all too familiar because you recognize them in yourself. These can be rooted out, but not by yourself; it requires a commitment to purity, holiness, and a dedication to Christlike living.

As Paul explains the qualifications and disqualifications for leaders, he makes a profound statement: *To the pure, all things are pure, but to the defiled and unbelieving, nothing is pure* (Titus 1:15). He is not just stating that lovers of good will find good even in an evil world, but he is also saying that if you are not a lover of good, you will have trouble seeing good in anything. Evil minds find evil in everything.

2. Change Your Thoughts and Attitudes

We all have people in our lives who test our patience. Lovers of good look for redemptive qualities instead of seeing the negative.

The following is an exercise to help you reframe negative thoughts and attitudes. In each numbered space below, write the name of a person you find especially grating (be honest; it will help you get the most out of this exercise).

Now practice seeing the good. In the three lettered spaces after each name, write a positive quality about him or her. Try to find qualities you even find admirable. Then spend a few moments associating the person you named with the qualities you listed. The goal is to think about the person's good qualities when you think about him or her rather than the qualities that annoy you. A lover of good does this by habit. Build that habit.

1. _____

   a. _____

   b. _____

   c. _____

2. _____

   a. _____

   b. _____

   c. _____

3. _____

a. _____

b. _____

c. _____

Now let's try it with things in life that bother you. Repeat the above exercise, but this time list three circumstances that particularly irritate you – for example, heavy traffic or loud neighbors. In the lettered spaces, write three ways you can use that circumstance for good. For example, heavy traffic gives you time to listen to an audiobook, listen to relaxing music, or meditate on Scripture and pray. I'm sure you can think of many more ideas. It may seem difficult at first, but with practice, you will be finding good in even the worst situations.

1. _____

   a. _____

   b. _____

   c. _____

2. _____

   a. _____

   b. _____

   c. _____

3. _____

   a. _____

   b. _____

   c. _____

Rooting out negativity doesn't mean that people will never irritate you, nor does it mean you'll be happy in all of life's situations. But it does mean you won't spend as much time in a negative state of mind. You will find joy even when you meet trials of various kinds, knowing that hardships are designed to build spiritual maturity (James 1:2-4) so that your faith is genuine (1 Peter 1:7).

3. Fill Your Mind with Good Thoughts

We (the authors) live in a desert climate. Our summers are quite hot, but even in the hottest months, we are occasionally surprised by cool temperatures for a day or two. As I (B. W.) walked with a friend on one of those unseasonably cool days, I commented, "What fantastic weather we are having!" My friend grumbled, "Yeah, for now." His disparaging comment revealed his negative outlook.

Lovers of good refuse to have cynical attitudes. People who have the character of Christ see good in something good, such as the enjoyment of a cool day after many hot days, but lovers of bad see only negative things. These two outlooks highlight differences in the condition of the heart. Lovers of good have hearts filled with gratitude because they find ultimate joy in Christ. For lovers of bad, Christ is not enough.

How do we cure ourselves of a negative outlook? Paul gives us the prescription in Philippians 4:8: *Finally, brothers, whatever is true, whatever is honorable, whatever is just, whatever is pure, whatever is lovely, whatever is commendable, if there is any excellence, if there is anything worthy of praise, think about these things.*

Paul is not merely recommending that we think happy thoughts, but he is challenging us to change our entire outlook on life. He is prescribing an overhaul of our attitudes. Lovers of good have eliminated negative outlooks in exchange for seeing truth, nobility, rightness, purity, loveliness, admirability, excellence, and praiseworthiness. It will take time and patience to master Philippians 4:8 because it is not a simple task to reframe your thinking. In fact, you can't do it on your own. But there is someone who is true, honorable, just, pure, lovely, commendable, excellent, and worthy of praise. If you will put your faith in Him, Jesus, to renew your mind through the power of His Spirit (Romans 8:5; 12:2; Titus 3:5), He will empower you to be a lover of good.

4. Choose to Do Good

Lovers of good don't just separate themselves from the bad by changing their thoughts and attitudes, but they also pursue good through their actions. They find good, they assume good, and they *do* good. The best way to train yourself to do good is by taking the Golden Rule seriously. In Luke 6:31, Jesus tells us to *do* to others as we would have them do to us.

Try this exercise: In the spaces below, list three things you would like people to do for you.

1. _____

   _____

2. _____

_____

3. _____

_____

Now how can you do each of those for another person? Go and do them!

Jesus doesn't stop with the Golden Rule. In the next few verses (Luke 6:32-36), He tells us to love those who don't love us, to do good to those who are not good to us, and to lend to those whom we do not expect will repay us. He summarizes these actions by saying, *Love your enemies.* Love our enemies! That idea is completely contrary to our human nature.

How do we learn to love our enemies? By acting like we already love them. This is not a call to phoniness or duplicity. It's putting the Golden Rule into practice and trusting that your heart will catch up with actions. In doing this, you will slowly build within yourself a habit of tolerance.

Think of the person you have the most trouble tolerating. Write his or her name below.

Name: _____

Ask yourself: If I accepted this person just as he or she is, how would I behave? What would I actually do?

Now go and behave as you just imagined. Do not wait for your "enemy" to change. Instead, be obedient to Christ and love him or her just as he or she is.

While implementing the Golden Rule, have an

attitude of generosity and kindness. Even a person with very little material wealth has wealth he or she can give away every day.[30] You can:

- give smiles to everyone

- give gratitude

- give honor and credit

- give time to worthy causes

- give hope

- give encouragement

- give uplifting words

- give pleasant greetings and responses

- give forgiveness

God richly blesses those who gladly give to others. Jesus said, *Give, and it will be given to you. Good measure, pressed down, shaken together, running over, will be put into your lap. For with the measure you use it will be measured back to you* (Luke 6:38). If we give such things as kindness and forgiveness to others, they will come back to us in full measure. This is an exciting truth, but it should not be the only motivation for doing and loving good. Lovers of good choose to do good because they know their good works give glory to their Father in heaven (Matthew 5:16).

My (B. W.) sister Donica is a true lover of good. She can find good in anything. For instance, she has suffered severe back pain for many years and has every reason

---

30   Gene Getz, *The Measure of a Man* (Ventura, CA: Regal, 2004), 205.

to complain when her back hurts. Yet she chooses to focus on the times when she's *not* in pain. A devout follower of Christ, she finds positives in even the worst situations. But she does more than that.

There was a time in my life when I was backslidden. I was far from Christ and Donica saw it. She put aside her regular tendency to see the good in me and wrote me a letter that was scathing, yet drenched in love. She called me out on every one of my sinful ways. She did not take it easy on me, but exposed my terrible actions. The letter really shook me. In fact, it devastated me. But I needed that letter. It became my impetus to repent, turn away from my sin, and turn back toward Christ, and I love her for it.

My sister knew an important truth: sometimes being a lover of good means being a hater of bad.

5. Love God Wholeheartedly

One day, an expert in the law stood up to trick Jesus, asking Him a question: *Teacher, which is the great commandment in the Law?* (Matthew 22:36). Jesus summarized the entire Old Testament in two commandments: *You shall love the Lord your God with all your heart and with all your soul and with all your mind. This is the great and first commandment. And a second is like it: You shall love your neighbor as yourself* (Matthew 22:37-39).

The way to love good is to follow the law of Christ. Gene Getz wrote, "The extent to which I love God and reflect that love by doing his will revealed in the word of God is also the degree to which I love what is good.

Consequently, the real questions I must face are, do I *really* love God? How *much* do I really love God?"[31] As you choose to love God wholeheartedly and love others genuinely, it will be hard *not* to be a lover of good, because loving good is a byproduct of loving God.

Jesus Is Our Model of Loving Good

Jesus was not only a lover of good, but His very character and nature were and are good. Beyond good. Perfect. So it is no wonder that He would see good when others might see otherwise. His disciples, for instance, were *indignant* when Martha's sister, Mary, poured expensive perfumed oil on Jesus' head in an act of devotion and worship. The disciples, noble in their own eyes, asked, *Why this waste?* (Matthew 26:8). They voiced their opinion that ointment could be sold for a good sum of money and given to the poor (v. 9).

What was a waste to the disciples was *a beautiful thing* (v. 10) to Jesus. Mary unknowingly anointed Jesus' body, preparing Him for His impending death and burial (v. 12). He recognized that she was doing something good, something beautiful, something that would be remembered. Jesus said, *Truly, I say to you, wherever this gospel is proclaimed in the whole world, what she has done will also be told in memory of her* (v. 13).

We are not perfect like Jesus, but as we put our faith in Him, He will help us see as He sees. Trust in Him to make you more and more like Him, and you, too, can be a lover of good in every person and in every situation.

---

31   Getz, *Measure*, 205.

Chapter 10

Be Holy

God calls all believers to live holy lives. He is holy, and we are to be holy in all we do (1 Peter 1:15). It is no wonder that Paul expected church leaders to be holy (see Titus 1:8). They are the ones who are entrusted with the responsibility to shepherd God's flock (1 Peter 5:1-2). If they are not pursuing godliness, they won't be able to inspire the same pursuit in others.

Christians commonly define holy as "set apart." This is true of the Greek word *hagios*, which is translated "holy" more than 220 times in the New Testament. But in his letter to Titus, Paul used a slightly different word: *hosios*. This word only appears eight times in the New Testament. In addition to "set apart," it means "sanctioned by the supreme law of God and nature; pious; devout."[32] It is used in Acts 2:27 and 13:35 to describe the supreme holiness of Jesus, our High Priest,

---

32 William Mounce, *Mounce's Complete Expository Dictionary of Old and New Testament Words* (Grand Rapids: Zondervan, 2006), 1,227.

who is utterly *hosios* because He is without sin and is completely pure.[33]

Our Call to Holiness

Why would Paul call leaders to such a high level of holiness? There are at least six reasons.

First, God commands it of every Christian leader. In 2 Timothy 2:19, Paul says this of every worker who is approved by God: *Let everyone who names the name of the Lord depart from iniquity.* If we are to be ready for every good work and useful to the Master, we must put aside all sin and cleanse ourselves from what is dishonorable. If we do, we will be *a vessel for honorable use, set apart as holy* (2 Timothy 2:21).

Second, holiness demonstrates that we are conformed to the character of God.[34] We are created in God's image. Therefore, we are capable of reflecting God's character.

Third, holy leaders are examples of morality for those they lead. God sets the standard for morality. He is both just and merciful. He cares deeply for every one of His followers. Leaders should do the same. They should model morality that is above what the world calls moral. They should be self-sacrificing. They should abstain from unholy talk, thoughts, and actions. They should strive daily to make themselves devout followers of Christ.

The fourth reason Paul requires Christian leaders to be holy is so all decisions will be directed by God

---

33   Mounce, *Dictionary*, 338.

34   Jerry Bridges, *The Pursuit of Holiness* (Colorado Springs: NavPress, 2006), 9.

and led by the Holy Spirit. Holy leaders trust God when weighing options, and they choose actions that honor God (see Job 1:8). God may choose any number of ways to guide Christian leaders, but we can always count on His Word to light our path (Psalm 119:105).

Fifth, Christian leaders who are not holy cannot properly shepherd God's flock. For instance, how can a porn-addicted pastor lead a church to sexual purity? Leaders who defy God's commands both openly and privately cannot genuinely edify their followers. Paul requires leaders who will uphold the Word of God. These are holy leaders.

Finally, holy leaders follow God's will. Peter says that a sign of holiness is to not conform to the evil desires we had when we lived in ignorance. When we reflect God's holiness, we cannot help but follow His will. We will be moral as He is moral, just as He is just, and merciful as He is merciful.

We cannot be holy without the help of the Holy Spirit, who is always there to help us follow God's will (John 16:13) and to convict our hearts when we don't (John 16:8).

Reflecting Christ's Holiness

Becoming holy (our sanctification) is a progressive work. As we grow in our holiness, we become less and less shackled by sin and more and more like Christ in our lives.[35] This lifelong process is affected by both God and us. To be sure, we do not have equal roles, nor do we work in the same way, but Scripture makes

---

35   Wayne Grudem, *Bible Doctrine* (Grand Rapids: Zondervan, 1999), 326.

it clear that part of becoming holy is left in our hands (see Philippians 2:12). Noted theologian Wayne Grudem states, "The fact that Scripture emphasizes the role that we play in sanctification (with all the moral commands of the New Testament), makes it appropriate to teach that God calls us to cooperate with him in this activity."[36] We must do our part.

So how do we do our part in the sanctification process? Following are four biblical ways to reflect God's holiness.

1. Read God's Word and Let God's Word Read You

In John 17:17, Jesus prayed for His disciples (and for us): *Sanctify them in the truth; your word is truth.* He is asking His Father to set apart His followers for holy service. He is also describing the means of sanctification: the Word of God.

When we read God's Word with a heart to have it read us, God transforms us. This work of the Spirit takes place because *the Word of God is living and active, sharper than any two-edged sword, piercing to the division of soul and spirit, of joints and of marrow, and discerning the thoughts and intentions of the heart* (Hebrews 4:12).

Many pastors and church leaders may read their Bibles, but much of their reading is *in preparation.* They're preparing for a sermon or for a Bible study. All their Bible reading is focused on what they are preaching, not

---

36   Grudem, *Doctrine*, 331.

on what they are becoming in Christ. Every Christian leader needs a set time, apart from sermon or Bible study preparation, to read and meditate on God's precepts and delight in His statutes (Psalm 119:15-16). When we do so, our souls will be refreshed (Psalm 19:7), our eyes will be enlightened (Psalm 19:8), and we will find protection from sin's domination (Psalm 19:12-14).

As we allow Scripture to shape us, we will think and behave in new and right ways. We will *put off [our] old self, which belongs to [our] former manner of life*, and we become *renewed in the spirit of [our] minds* (Ephesians 4:22-23). This renewal transforms us so we can *put on the new self, created after the likeness of God in true righteousness and holiness* (v. 24). This process of sanctification is impossible without a daily commitment to reading and conforming our lives to God's Word.

2. Have a Firm Conviction That God Wants You to Be Holy

God reminds us throughout Scripture to *be holy, for I am holy* (e.g., Leviticus 11:44). He is quite clear that our sanctification is His will for us (1 Corinthians 1:2; 1 Thessalonians 4:3, 7; 2 Timothy 1:9). Scripture makes known that God truly desires our holiness, but an even more powerful statement was made by Christ's actions: He *died* so that we can be holy. Paul said, *And you, who once were alienated and hostile in mind, doing evil deeds, he has now reconciled in his body of flesh by his death, in order to present you holy and blameless and above reproach before him* (Colossians 1:21-22).

We need to have the conviction that God wants us to be holy, and then we need to live out this conviction.

3. Develop Convictions for "Tolerable" Sins

It is essential to have a zero-tolerance policy for all sin. In *The Pursuit of Holiness,* Jerry Bridges wrote, "[Our] problem is that we do not take sin seriously. We have mentally categorized sins into that which is unacceptable and that which may be tolerated a bit."[37] The unacceptable sins are obvious, such as stealing (Exodus 20:15), adultery (Exodus 20:14), sexual immorality (1 Thessalonians 4:3), lying (Ephesians 4:25), and murder (Exodus 20:13).

The "tolerable" sins are less obvious. Such sins include:

- unforgiveness

- white lies

- fudging on taxes

- sins we justify (stealing office supplies from work, breaking speed limit laws, sharing streaming media account passwords with others, etc.)

- off-color jokes

- music with explicit lyrics or themes

- movies that glamorize sin

- overindulgence/gluttony

---

37   Bridges, *Holiness*, 5.

- coveting others' status, church size, or influence

Tolerable sins are still sins. As soon as we start ranking sins as less or more "sinful," we become tolerant of sin in general. If you are tolerating even "small" sins in your life, you are not moving toward sanctification but from it.

Not only do "tolerable" sins need to be intolerable, but we must be aware of sins lurking in the so-called gray area. Paul gave the Corinthians a five-part filter with which to gauge whether a particular thought, action, or attitude is right or wrong in God's eyes.[38]

Question 1: Does it help me physically? spiritually? mentally?

> *"All things are lawful for me," but not all things are helpful* (1 Corinthians 6:12).

Question 2: Does it bring me under its power?

> *"All things are lawful for me," but I will not be dominated by anything* (1 Corinthians 6:12).

Question 3: Does it harm others or make them stumble?

> *Therefore, if food makes my brother stumble, I will never eat meat, lest I make my brother stumble* (1 Corinthians 8:13).

---

38   Adapted from Bridges, *Holiness*, 69-70.

Question 4: Does it build others up and benefit them?

> *"All things are lawful," but not all things build up. Let no one seek his own good, but the good of his neighbor* (1 Corinthians 10:23-24).

Question 5: Does it glorify God?

> *So, whether you eat or drink, or whatever you do, do it all to the glory of God* (1 Corinthians 10:31).

Using these five questions, one can determine if a thought, action, or attitude is best avoided. Try it. Think about your favorite television show and ask yourself:

1. Does it help me physically? spiritually? mentally?

2. Does it bring me under its power?

3. Does it harm others or make them stumble?

4. Does it build others up and benefit them?

5. Does it glorify God?

Many people love to watch football. *We* love to watch football. There is nothing inherently wrong with watching a football game on television or in person. The problem is when the game conflicts with your pursuit of holiness.

Consider this scenario: John Churchgoer is a huge 49ers fan. This Sunday his beloved 49ers take on the Dallas Cowboys. His brother-in-law, Carl No-Church, is a devoted Cowboys supporter. Carl has invited John over to watch the game. Kickoff is at 10:00 a.m. on Sunday. John, who is striving to be holy, must decide whether or not to accept Carl's invitation. He really wants to go, but he uses Paul's filter.

Q1: Does it help me physically? spiritually? mentally?

John instinctively says, "Watching football is a great stress reliever. It helps me mentally." Then he realizes he is justifying his desire to watch the game. Watching the game with Carl means missing his time with the assembly of the saints. It is *not* beneficial spiritually.

John could stop right here, but for the sake of demonstrating Paul's filter, we continue.

Q2: Does it bring me under its power?

John was strongly considering missing church to watch the game. He may not be fully under its power, but that's a red flag, and he must be diligent about keeping his priorities in order. When he was ruled by his "old self" (Ephesians 4:22), he never missed a game. Football was an idol in his life. He has seen the power that football can have over him.

Q3: Does it harm others or make them stumble?

It would not directly harm Carl if John went over to watch the game. However, John would be missing a wonderful opportunity. John could say to Carl, "I'd love to watch the game with you. How about we DVR it, you come to church with me, and we watch it afterward?"

Who knows? Carl may find Jesus and need to change his last name!

Q4: Does it build others up and benefit them?

It might. John can use this time with Carl to strengthen their relationship.

Q5: Does it glorify God?

Because John would be choosing football over communing with the saints, it does not glorify God. Again, John could DVR the game and watch it with Carl later in the day.

The five-question filter can give you insight into all aspects of your life. We all know that viewing pornography is sinful, but what about certain television shows? You may not feel that your favorite show is harmful physically, spiritually, or mentally, but if you find it unthinkable to miss an episode, then maybe it's becoming an idol.

The five questions can even apply to the friends you keep. We know that bad company corrupts good morals (1 Corinthians 15:33). Subject your close relationships to Paul's five-part filter and see if they are relationships that build you up.

4. Learn to Say "No"

Paul said that *the grace of God* trains us to *renounce ungodliness and worldly passions, and to live self-controlled, upright, and godly lives in the present age* (Titus 2:11-12). Following are several things to say no to.

Say no to sins that easily entangle you. We all have sins that we have trouble resisting. We give these sins power by reframing them as vices, weaknesses, or shortcomings. I (B. W.) have a Christian friend who is addicted to chewing tobacco. He says, "Dipping is my vice" in an attempt to avoid acknowledging the grip that nicotine has over him. He implies that he owns the vice, but the vice owns him. Because we are empowered by the grace of God, we have just as much power over our vices as we do over any other sin.

Say no to making exceptions. God has no commandments that should be followed "most of the time." We must not fall into the dangerous habit of allowing ourselves to sin "just this once." Jerry Bridges put it this way: "Because we are unwilling to pay the price of saying no to our desires, we tell ourselves that we will indulge only once more and tomorrow will be different. Deep inside we know that tomorrow it will be even more difficult to say no, but we don't dwell on this fact."[39]

Anyone who has been addicted to pornography knows how easy it is to stop but how difficult it is to stop and stay stopped. The lie of "this is the last time" eases guilt and minimizes sin. This kind of thinking keeps us tethered to iniquity.

Finally, say yes to obedience. Peter said, *As obedient children, do not be conformed to the passions of your former ignorance, but as he who called you is holy, you also be holy in all your conduct* (1 Peter 1:14-15). There

---

39   Bridges, *Holiness*, 107.

is an inseparable connection between holiness and obedience. The two *always* go hand in hand.

The Bible is filled with exhortations to help us live devout and holy lives. The following exhortations from Colossians 3 exemplify the life that God calls us to live. Take a few moments and examine yourself. Below you will find a list of sins that we are to put to death, followed by virtues that we are to exemplify. Give yourself a check mark if you think you are walking in full obedience to God's Word. Give yourself a minus (–) if you are convicted to grow in this area.

Have you put *to death* the following?

_____ sexual immorality (v. 5)

_____ impurity (v. 5)

_____ passion (v. 5)

_____ evil desire (v. 5)

_____ covetousness (v. 5)

_____ anger (v. 8)

_____ wrath (v. 8)

_____ malice (v. 8)

_____ slander (v. 8)

_____ obscene talk (v. 8)

_____ lies (v. 9)

Have you put *on* the following?

_____ a compassionate heart (v. 12)

_____ kindness (v. 12)

_____ humility (v. 12)

_____ meekness (v. 12)

_____ patience (v. 12)

_____ bearing with one another (v. 13)

_____ forgiveness (v. 13)

_____ love (v. 14)

_____ the peace of Christ (v. 15)

_____ thankfulness (v. 15)

_____ the word of Christ (v. 16)

_____ teaching one another (v. 16)

_____ admonishing one another (v. 16)

_____ singing psalms and hymns (v. 16)

_____ doing everything in the name of the Lord Jesus (v. 17)

Obedience and holiness are developed intentionally through diligence. John Owen said, "Without a sincere and diligent effort in every area of obedience, there will be no successful mortification of any one besetting sin.[40] If we allow some "small" sins to go unchecked,

---

40   John Owen, *Temptation and Sin* (Regent College, 1983), 40.

it becomes easier and easier for us to allow other sins into our lives. God wants us to be obedient in *all* areas of our lives, and "the more we succeed in saying no to our sinful desires, the easier it becomes to say no."[41]

Holiness is a serious qualification for leadership. Even more important, holiness is a serious qualification for God. He says, *Be holy, for I am holy* (Leviticus 11:44). Those you serve need a leader who bears the image of Christ. You cannot lead them to a holy God if holiness is not alive in you. So be holy.

Jesus Is Our Model of Holiness

Jesus was tempted in every area of His personal life, just like us, *yet without sin* (Hebrews 4:15). He remained sinless throughout His life, *holy, innocent, unstained, separated from sinners* (Hebrews 7:26).

Nothing defiled Jesus. No one in His day would dare touch a person with leprosy, because the disease was highly contagious, and touching a leper made a person ceremonially unclean. But Jesus did. A leper knelt before Him and said, *"Lord, if you will, you can make me clean." And Jesus stretched out his hand and touched him, saying, "I will; be clean"* (Matthew 8:2-3). Rather than the leper's disease and uncleanliness going into Jesus, Jesus imparted His healing and cleanliness into the leper.

As we follow Jesus' example of holiness, we must not let the world defile us. We live in the world, but we are to *set [our] minds on things above, not on things*

---

41   Owen, *Temptation*, 40.

that are on earth (Colossians 3:2). Rather than letting the uncleanliness of the world affect us, we are to send Christ's purity into it, blessing those who persecute us (Romans 12:14), refusing to retaliate when we're wronged (v. 19), showing kindness to our enemies (v. 20), and overcoming evil with good (v. 21).

As we follow Christ's example of holiness, we will be *blameless and innocent, children of God without blemish in the midst of a crooked and twisted generation, among whom [we] shine as lights in the world* (Philippians 2:15).

Appendix

Character Trait Assessment (CTA)

The purpose of this assessment is to help measure a leader's character. The CTA should be filled out by the leader and three individuals who are familiar with the leader's life and/or ministry.

Leader's Name _____

For each character trait below, write the number in the space that describes how the trait is manifested in the leader's life. Please be honest. This assessment will help the leader become aware of areas in his/her life that need growth.

Key:

5 = Strongly Developed
4 = Mostly Developed
3 = Partly Developed
2 = Needs Much Improvement
1 = Nonexistent

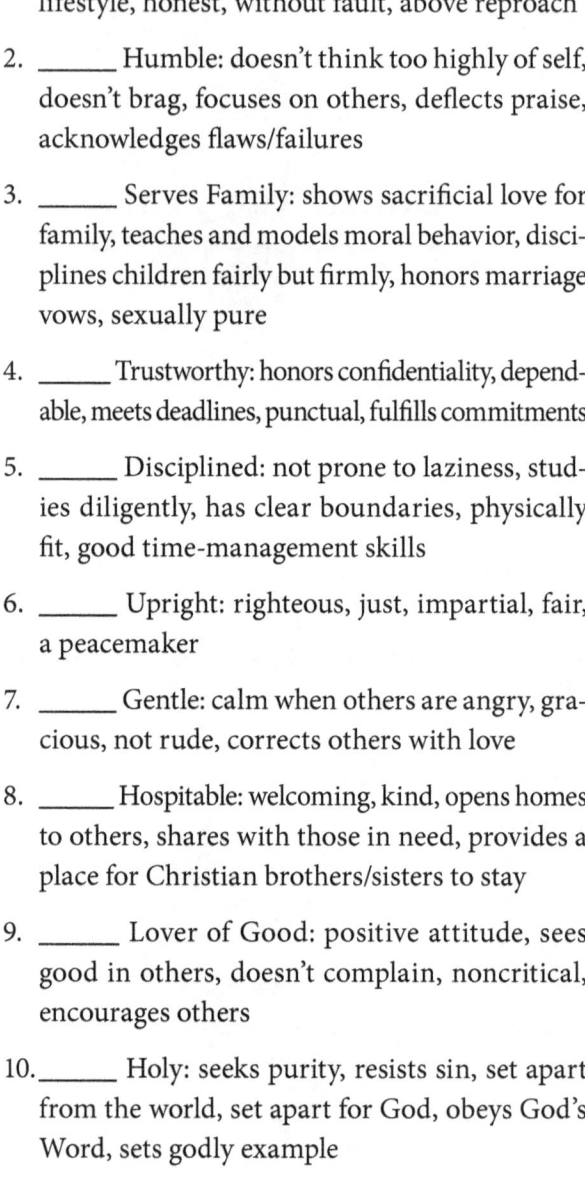

1. _____ Blameless: follows rules, obeys laws, godly lifestyle, honest, without fault, above reproach

2. _____ Humble: doesn't think too highly of self, doesn't brag, focuses on others, deflects praise, acknowledges flaws/failures

3. _____ Serves Family: shows sacrificial love for family, teaches and models moral behavior, disciplines children fairly but firmly, honors marriage vows, sexually pure

4. _____ Trustworthy: honors confidentiality, dependable, meets deadlines, punctual, fulfills commitments

5. _____ Disciplined: not prone to laziness, studies diligently, has clear boundaries, physically fit, good time-management skills

6. _____ Upright: righteous, just, impartial, fair, a peacemaker

7. _____ Gentle: calm when others are angry, gracious, not rude, corrects others with love

8. _____ Hospitable: welcoming, kind, opens homes to others, shares with those in need, provides a place for Christian brothers/sisters to stay

9. _____ Lover of Good: positive attitude, sees good in others, doesn't complain, noncritical, encourages others

10. _____ Holy: seeks purity, resists sin, set apart from the world, set apart for God, obeys God's Word, sets godly example

CTA Scoring

Character Trait	Self-Evaluation	Evaluator 1	Evaluator 2	Evaluator 3	Total
1. Blameless					
2. Humble					
3. Serves Family					
4. Trustworthy					
5. Discipled					
6. Upright					
7. Gentle					
8. Hospitable					
9. Lover of Good					
10. Holy					

1. In the "Self-Evaluation" column, record the number you assigned for each dimension of character.

2. In the Evaluator 1, 2, and 3 columns, record each evaluator's score in the proper row.

3. Now add the lines across and record the sum in the "Total" column.

Using the Results

CTA Scoring

Christ exemplified perfect character in every area of His life. As you strive to be like Him, you will become a Christlike leader in your home and in your church. The results of the CTA will help you focus on the areas of your character that need the most improvement. While it is vital to develop Christlike character in all ten areas that are presented in this book, for the purposes of this exercise, focus on the three areas in which you scored the lowest. As you complete the following exercise, be sure to do so with honesty and humility. Your goal is to grow, not to impress yourself.

Questions

1. Which three character dimensions had the lowest score?

2. What surprised you about the results?

3. Were there traits in which you scored yourself differently than your evaluators? Why do you think this was the case?

Note: It is our experience that your evaluators will score you more accurately than you will score yourself. Your close friends can see your fruit much more clearly than you can see your own, as each person is known by his fruit (Luke 6:44).

Actions to Take

Focus on the three areas of your character that need the most improvement and take the following actions:

1. Pray. You cannot grow in Christlike character on your own; you need God's help and power. Pray regularly for God to shape your character and to make you like Christ.

2. Ask for accountability. Invite your spouse or another believer to help you, and give the person permission to let you know when you're missing the mark.

3. Read and reread the chapters that relate to your

weak character areas. For each chapter, be sure to answer the questions for personal reflection located in the Study Guide. These questions are designed to help you apply biblical principles to your life to help you grow in Christlikeness.

4. Be on constant watch for opportunities to practice the character traits. If you are vigilant, you will see many chances to practice as God shapes you and develops you. Take advantage of these growth opportunities.

5. Commit to a lifelong pattern of growth in Christlike character, trusting that *he who began a good work in you will bring it to completion at the day of Jesus Christ* (Philippians 1:6).

Note: Keep in mind that the CTA is simply a tool to help give you insight into your character.

New Beginnings for Those Who Fall

This book has described the character needed to be leaders of God's household. But what about those of us who have already had a moral failure by which our character failings seem to disqualify us from kingdom service? Is there any hope for us?

The gospel says yes! It redeems and restores what has been destroyed. It is the quintessential message of love, grace, and forgiveness. It proves through resounding evidence that God is not like us, yet He sent His Son to us to become like one of us to save us from our own self-destruction. This is why the gospel is such good news – *like cold water to a thirsty soul* (Proverbs 25:25).

The heart of the gospel's message recognizes that people fail, but God fixes. People ruin, but God remedies. If God kept a record of our iniquities, we would never be worthy to be used for Him and could never stand before Him forgiven (Psalm 130:3). And so God does for us what we are unable to do in our weakness (Romans 5:6; 8:3), paying the penalty price of our sin and removing the powerful preeminence of sin. Paul said, *Where sin increased, grace abounded all the more* so that grace *might reign through righteousness leading to eternal life through Jesus Christ our Lord* (Romans 5:20-21). What amazing grace – grace so amazing that God gives every repentant heart second chances, third chances, and as many chances as it takes and will use any humble, truly repentant vessel, even broken ones, to make a kingdom difference with his or her life!

Despite our past failings, God looks forward. If we repent of our sin, accept His correction, and follow His leading, we can rise from past failings and say, *By the grace of God I am what I am, and his grace toward me was not in vain* (1 Corinthians 15:10). We may doubt ourselves, but let us not doubt what God is willing and able to do with those who are broken. There is hope, and it is only in Him. *Hope in the LORD! For with the LORD there is steadfast love, and with him is plentiful redemption. . . . Blessed be the Lord, who daily bears us up; God is our salvation* (Psalm 130:7; 68:19).

Because the gospel is alive, the past is the past, today is a new day, and the future is looking quite spectacular (Jeremiah 29:11)! Receive the hope that Christ gives you and put your faith in Him to begin again.

Questions for Group Discussion and Personal Reflection

This study guide will help you review, assess, and apply what you have learned in this book. Each chapter contains five questions that can be used for group discussion or personal reflection. We pray that this guide serves as a tool for spiritual transformation as you seek to be a leader who presents yourself to God as one approved (2 Timothy 2:15).

Chapter 1: Be Blameless

Your character matters. It matters more than the work you do, and more than the size of your ministry. Heading Paul's list of qualifications for church leaders is blamelessness. If a leader is not above reproach and his character can be impugned, he has no business being in church leadership. The call to blamelessness doesn't mean that we are sinless, but it does mean that we have a reputation of godly character without cause for someone to accuse us on moral grounds. Do you strive to avoid even the appearance of evil in your life?

Questions for Group Discussion or Personal Reflection

1. The pursuit of godliness must be a leader's highest priority. Read the following verses from 1 Timothy that emphasize godly living: 2:2; 4:7-8; 5:4; 6:3; 6:6; 6:11. How might you apply each of these verses in your life? Be specific.

2. One of the authors shared a resolution he made in his effort to pursue blamelessness. His resolution was created as a guardrail to help him keep a close watch on himself (Ephesians 4:16). Create your own resolution that will serve as a guardrail to help you stay on the path of godliness. After you have created your final draft, place it in a prominent area to remind you of your resolution to be above reproach.

3. Church leaders model to those in their congregations how to live and behave. Therefore, we must do such things as (1) practice what we preach, (2) obey the laws, (3) tell the truth, (4) avoid gossip, (5) stand strong in faith amid trials and tribulations, and (6) live a godly lifestyle in the community, at church, and at home. Describe one specific way you can make an improvement in each of these six areas.

4. How does Jesus model blamelessness?

5. How will you specifically cultivate blamelessness in your (1) marriage, (2) household, and (3) ministry?

Chapter 2: Be Humble

Jesus put God first and was perfectly submitted to Him. While contemplating the path of obedience set before Him, He prayed to His father, *Not as I will, but as you will* (Matthew 26:39). Jesus was a humble servant who relied entirely on His Father, never acting on His own (John 5:19). God wants us to cultivate humility and become servants who obediently follow the will of God. Allow the Holy Spirit to reveal any areas of self-reliance that need to be put to death. Then have faith that Jesus will reshape your heart so you can walk in Christlike humility.

Questions for Group Discussion or Personal Reflection

1. Humble leaders are servant leaders. Describe five ways you can serve those you lead. Be specific. How can you put your ideas into action?

2. What are the characteristics of humble people according to this chapter? Why do you think it is essential for leaders to be humble?

3. Do you have a modest opinion of yourself? To evaluate your opinion, answer the following questions honestly. To what extent do you:

   - feel superior to those who work for you?

   - fail to regularly acknowledge the debt you owe to your mentors and to others?

   - denigrate the motives and accomplishments of others?

   - expect others to serve you or defer to you?

   - put your own success ahead of the success of others?

   - behave in ways that seem egocentric to those around you?

   What will you do to make sure you count others as more significant than yourself (Philippians 2:3)?

4. How does Jesus model humility?

5. How will you specifically cultivate humility in your (1) marriage, (2) household, and (3) ministry?

Chapter 3: Be a Steward of Your Family

Spiritual leadership begins at home. If you cannot manage your household well, the Bible says you are unqualified to lead His household (1 Timothy 3:4-5). Since your home is the proving ground for church leadership, it is vital to be a spouse and a parent who loves and serves like Christ Jesus.

Questions for Group Discussion or Personal Reflection

1. Husbands: What does it look like to love your wife as Christ loved the church and gave Himself up for her? In what ways can you start loving your wife like that today?

   Wives: What does it look like to love your husband and submit to him? In what ways can you start loving your husband like that today?

2. Pornography is a scourge on our society. It ruins the lives of believers as well as unbelievers. List every way you can think of in which pornography can and does destroy lives.

3. Church overseers must have nonnegotiable expectations in the home. Create a list of at least seven expectations for your household. You may

draw from the list of expectations given in this chapter or create some of your own. How will you lead your family to meet these expectations?

4. How does Jesus model family stewardship?

5. How will you specifically cultivate being a steward of your family in your (1) marriage, (2) household, and (3) ministry?

Chapter 4: Be Trustworthy

Would people say that you are trustworthy? Trust is a fragile thing. It is easily broken, and once broken, it's difficult to repair. Sometimes it is never repaired. Trustworthy leaders know a valuable secret: keeping trust is easier than regaining trust.

Questions for Group Discussion or Personal Reflection

1. Reliable people keep their word, keep a schedule, and are punctual. Why do you think a church leader needs to excel in these three areas? How do you fare?

2. How do white lies or small lies destroy credibility just as much as big lies do?

3. Why must competency go hand-in-hand with honesty? In what ways are people who are incompetent in their areas of leadership or expertise untrustworthy?

4. How does Jesus model trustworthiness?

5. How will you specifically cultivate trustworthiness in your (1) marriage, (2) household, and (3) ministry?

Chapter 5: Be Disciplined

Every church leader must be disciplined. You are a steward of God's possession and God's people. You are responsible to care for the spiritual needs of the flock. Such care cannot be administered haphazardly or without intentionality. You must be disciplined to handle the things of God. Discipline is required in both your private life and in the responsibilities to which you attend at church.

Questions for Group Discussion or Personal Reflection

1. Describe two areas in your life in which you lack self-discipline. What can you specifically do to make improvements in these areas?

2. What are some potential problems that might emerge in a church through the leadership of an undisciplined person?

3. Describe three small changes you can make in your routine to improve your health (e.g., eat smaller portions, park farther away from the building, go for a walk after a meal). When will you start making these changes?

4. How does Jesus model discipline?

5. How will you specifically cultivate discipline in your (1) marriage, (2) household, and (3) ministry?

Chapter 6: Be Upright

The prophet Micah lamented the loss of godliness in his day, cataloging the sins of both the northern and southern kingdoms. These sins included idolatry (Micah 1:7), the belief that personal sacrifice satisfied God's justice (6:6-7), and corrupt business practices and violence (6:10-12). It is no wonder that he cried out, *The godly has perished from the earth, and there is no one upright among mankind* (7:2). We are also living in ungodly times, seeing more and more the fulfillment of Paul's prophecy of godlessness in the last days (2 Timothy 3:1-7). Church leaders must be upright and holy (Titus 1:8) *in the midst of a crooked and twisted generation*, shining *as lights in the world* (Philippians 2:15).

Questions for Group Discussion or Personal Reflection

1. How have you seen partiality cause problems in families, churches, or other organizations? Why is it essential to avoid favoritism in the church?

2. To make just decisions, we must pray for wisdom, seek godly counsel, seek God's Word, and look to glorify God. Think about a decision you are facing in your life or ministry. How might

the four steps above help you ensure that your decision is wise and godly?

3. The four G's of biblical restoration are: Glorify God, Get the log out of your eye, Gently restore, and Go be reconciled. The first two steps, glorify God and get the log out of your eye, are often overlooked in the peacemaking process. Why are these two steps important to take?

4. How does Jesus model uprightness?

5. How will you specifically cultivate uprightness in your (1) marriage, (2) household, and (3) ministry?

Chapter 7: Be Gentle

Jesus was *gentle and lowly in heart* (Matthew 11:29). The more we let His Spirit come alive in our lives, the more we will bear the fruit of love, joy, peace, patience, kindness, goodness, faithfulness, gentleness, and self-control (Galatians 5:22-23), becoming like Him in all our ways. May the people in your church and in your home be able to say that you are gentle and lowly in heart, returning harsh words with kindness and speaking the truth with love and grace.

Questions for Group Discussion or Personal Reflection

1. Paul disqualifies anyone from leadership who is not gentle. Why do you suppose he does this? Can

a leader be both strong and gentle? Give a biblical example of a leader who is strong yet gentle.

2. Solomon said, *A soft answer turns away wrath, but a harsh word stirs up anger* (Proverbs 15:1). Describe a situation from your experience in which your gentle answer deflected someone's anger. Now describe a situation in which your harsh words made someone's temper flare.

3. Why is it important to defend the gospel with gentleness rather than using aggressive tactics when sharing your faith amid opposition?

4. How does Jesus model gentleness?

5. How will you specifically cultivate gentleness in your (1) marriage, (2) household, and (3) ministry?

Chapter 8: Be Hospitable

God gives us a beautiful picture of hospitality. He prepares a dwelling house for us (Psalm 23:6). He is the King who invites us to His banqueting table (Song of Solomon 2:4). He is the Shepherd who feeds us spiritually through Christ and His Word (Psalm 23:3). He invites us into His presence, bringing us into spiritual blessings in heavenly places (Ephesians 1:3) and accepting us *in the Beloved* (Ephesians 1:6). We can be confident of the Lord's care and provision and the kindness He shows in receiving us into His own.

Questions for Group Discussion or Personal Reflection

1. When someone is shown hospitality, how is this person benefited? Do you intentionally show hospitality to those under your care?

2. Are you in the practice of opening your home to (1) other Christians, (2) itinerant preachers or missionaries, and (3) strangers? Why or why not?

3. What are some of the excuses some believers give for not helping those in need?

4. How does Jesus model hospitality?

5. How will you specifically cultivate hospitality in your (1) marriage, (2) household, and (3) ministry?

Chapter 9: Be a Lover of Good

Do you have a critical heart or a compassionate heart toward others and God? Do you speak words of complaint or words of gratitude? Christian leaders who are lovers of good love the good and refuse to grumble about the bad. They see the best in everyone and everything, displaying a positive attitude that reflects the mind of Christ. In essence, they are lovers of good because they are lovers of God.

Questions for Group Discussion
or Personal Reflection

1. Think about someone you find especially grating. You already know his or her negative qualities. Rather than describing these negative characteristics, describe three positive qualities about this person.

2. What is something (or who is someone) you complain about? Read Philippians 2:14-15. How does complaining affect your Christian testimony?

3. What is the connection between being a lover of good and being a lover of God?

4. How does Jesus model being a lover of good?

5. How will you specifically cultivate being a lover of good in your (1) marriage, (2) household, and (3) ministry?

Chapter 10: Be Holy

God commands us to be holy. Peter wrote, *As obedient children, do not be conformed to your passions of your former ignorance, but as he who called you is holy, you also be holy in all your conduct, since it is written, "You shall be holy, for I am holy"* (1 Peter 1:14-16).

A. W. Tozer asked, "Why don't we strive to be holy?"

His answer: "The major problem is that we like ourselves too much. We struggle to keep up a good front."[42] As you learn to have a proper perspective of yourself, walk in the will of God, and strive to be holy, your church family will reap the benefits. They will be served by a leader who is conformed to the character of God and obedient to follow His will.

Questions for Group Discussion or Personal Reflection

1. Read Colossians 3:5-9. Which sins from this list must be put to death in your life? What will it take to put them to death permanently?

2. What "tolerable" sins do you regularly engage in? How will you start removing these from your life? Be specific.

3. Every believer has a role to play in his or her sanctification. What is God's role? What is ours? What can you do to fulfill your role?

4. How does Jesus model holiness?

5. How will you specifically cultivate holiness in your (1) marriage, (2) household, and (3) ministry?

---

42   A. W. Tozer, *The Crucified Life* (Ventura, CA: Regal, 2011), 120.

About the Authors

D r. Johnson and Dr. Woolsey are founding members of Genesis College & Seminary, an international ministry serving thousands of inmates across the nation. Both have been faculty members at Christian colleges and universities. Johnson is blessed with four wonderful children and six cherished grandchildren, while Woolsey has two children who are a true blessing.

www.genesiscollegeandseminary.com

Other Similar Titles

Becoming a Leader Worth Following
by Fred Waggoner & Luke Kuepfer

"*Becoming A Leader Worth Following* is a must-read! Two transformational concepts for any leader I came away with are: 1) My leadership is limited – even Jesus lost Judas, and 2) Go deep with the few to impact the many – the ripple effect."

Dave Kauffman, Founder of Empowering Small Business; Author and Top 100 Keynote Speaker; Master DISC Trainer

"The authors have done a service to the body of Christ by reminding us that true leadership is God-focused, based on our character rather than gifts, and by being led by the Spirit of God."

Paul Hattaway, Director and Founder of Asia Harvest; Author of *Operation China*, *The Heavenly Man*, and *The China Chronicles*

Available where books are sold.

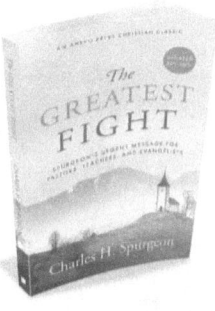

The Greatest Fight
by Charles H. Spurgeon

This book examines three things that are of utmost importance in this fight of faith. The first is *our armory*, which is the inspired Word of God. The second is *our army*, the church of the living God, which we must lead under our Lord's command. The third is *our strength*, by which we wear the armor and use the sword.

The message in this book, when originally presented by Charles Spurgeon in his final address to his own Pastor's College, was received rapturously and enthusiastically. It was almost immediately published and distributed around the world and in several languages. After Charles Spurgeon's death in 1892, 34,000 copies were printed and distributed to pastors and leaders in England through Mrs. Spurgeon's book fund. It is with great pleasure that we present this updated and very relevant book to the Lord's army of today.

Available where books are sold.

Words of Counsel
by Charles H. Spurgeon

Is there any occupation as profitable or rewarding as that of winning souls for Christ? It is a desirable employment, and the threshold for entry into this profession is set at a level any Christian may achieve – you must only love the Lord God with all your heart, soul, and mind; and your fellow man as yourself. This work is for all genuine Christians, of all walks of life. This is for you, fellow Christian.

Be prepared to be inspired, challenged, and convicted. Be prepared to weep, for the Holy Spirit may touch you deeply as you consider your coworkers, your neighbors, the children you know, and how much the Lord cares for these individuals. But you will also be equipped. Charles Spurgeon knew something about winning souls, and he holds nothing back as he shares biblical wisdom and practical application regarding the incredible work the Lord wants to do through His people to reach the lost.

Available where books are sold.

The Overcoming Life
by Dwight L. Moody

Overcome your greatest enemy, yourself.

Are you an overcomer? Or, are you plagued by little sins that easily beset you? Even worse, are you failing in your Christian walk, but refuse to admit and address it? No Christian can afford to dismiss the call to be an overcomer. The earthly cost is minor; the eternal reward is beyond measure.

Dwight L. Moody is a master at unearthing what ails us. He uses stories and humor to bring to light the essential principles of successful Christian living. Each aspect of overcoming is looked at from a practical and understandable angle. The solution Moody presents for our problems is not religion, rules, or other outward corrections. Instead, he takes us to the heart of the matter and prescribes biblical, God-given remedies for every Christian's life. Get ready to embrace genuine victory for today, and joy for eternity.

Available where books are sold.